THE PRIVATE ALBERT EINSTEIN

THE
PRIVATE
ALBERT
EINSTEIN

PETER A. BUCKY
In collaboration with Allen G. Weakland

ANDREWS and McMEEL
A Universal Press Syndicate Company
Kansas City

Designed by Cameron Poulter

Library of Congress Cataloging-in-Publication Data
Bucky, Peter A.
      The private Albert Einstein / Peter A. Bucky, in collaboration
with Allen G. Weakland.
            p.   cm.
      Includes index.
      ISBN 0-8362-7997-2 : $18.95
      1. Einstein, Albert, 1879-1955. 2. Physicists—Biography.
I. Einstein, Albert, 1879-1955. II. Weakland, Allen G. III. Title.
QC16.E5B83   1992
530'.092—dc20   92-4440
[B]   CIP

To my darling wife, Tina,

who contributed to this book

to a great degree

with important information.

Without her help

and constant encouragement,

this book would never

have been possible.

Contents

Einstein and the Buckys

The purpose of this book is not to add another to an interminable list of biographies of Albert Einstein. The purpose is, rather, to present an intimate sketch of the twentieth century's greatest scientist—a verbal photograph captured through the lens of a family who stood by Einstein's side both in Germany and in the United States.

Dr. Gustav Bucky, the patriarch of this family, was a lifelong friend and one of Einstein's personal physicians. Bucky's parents were wealthy and wanted their son, Gustav, to enter medicine to ensure the continuance of the family's prominence. But Gustav had other ideas, wishing instead to go into engineering. In the end, he compromised by entering radiology, since it was the closest thing in medicine to engineering. But the engineer in him was never far from the surface, and when he died he had 148 patents registered in his name. It was an activity he pursued mostly out of the love of pure science as evidenced by the fact that not even ten percent of his inventions were ever commercialized.

One that was, though, brought him renown. Bucky was a pioneer in X-ray technology and was the inventor of the Bucky Diaphragm, which eliminated the dissipation of X-rays on contact, thus making the X-raying of the human body more feasible.

Dr. Bucky's son, Peter A. Bucky, is president of Bucky X-Ray International, an international corporation that has exploited the inventions of his father and many of its own. When one reads today of customs agents cracking a narcotics ring, of postal inspectors X-raying parcels to find terrorist bombs, or of magical radiological advances in first-rate hospitals, it is likely that behind the scenes lurks Peter Bucky and his uncanny inventions.

But, aside from his professional success, Peter Bucky also retains a fund of personal knowledge about Prof. Albert Einstein— a knowledge gleaned from more than three decades of friendship during which Bucky and Einstein often drove together to vacation spots around the United States.

During these long rides together a bond was formed between the two men. Inhibitions disappeared and the resulting conversations, never before disclosed, grace the following pages.

The intimacy between the Bucky and Einstein families spanned two continents beginning in their German homeland and continuing in the United States, where they wound up. It was a friendship that was precarious for the Buckys, since Einstein, a Jew, was on the official Nazi hate list. The Gestapo, knowing of the connection, had the Buckys' telephone lines tapped to keep tabs on Einstein. Fortunately, even after a price was put on Einstein's head, the Nazis had to leave the Buckys alone because by this time they had become American citizens, a status that even the Gestapo respected in the pre-war days.

The friendship continued across the Atlantic when Einstein and his household moved to Princeton, New Jersey, a scant sixty miles from Manhattan, where the Buckys lived. The common German heritage of the two families certainly must have yielded a mutual comfort, for the friendship was so deep that, out of eleven people present at Einstein's private funeral, four were Buckys.

The friendship between Einstein and the elder Bucky stemmed from both a mutual interest in physical mechanics and similar character traits. Both men shunned publicity and resisted acclaim for their achievements.

Actually, the only time Einstein ever took out a joint patent with another inventor, his co-inventor was Dr. Bucky. The two men had developed an automatic adjustment of a photographic diaphragm that is still widely used in motion picture cameras. Bucky served as the practical partner while Einstein dealt with the theory. Unfortunately, neither Bucky nor Einstein had the slightest business acumen, and they never did anything with their patent. But the day their patent expired every major manufacturer of amateur movie cameras rushed to exploit their development.

Another little-known story demonstrating the bond between

Einstein and Dr. Bucky involves the only time that Einstein ever appeared in a United States court as an expert witness.

In 1936, Dr. Bucky had developed a medical camera that would take color pictures for a wide variety of medical applications. With this camera, a physician need not know anything about photography. The camera would automatically adjust itself to focus, frame, distance, exposure, and light—all simply by the insertion of one key.

In 1942, Dr. Bucky licensed the manufacture of the camera, and in the agreement he had inserted a clause clearly stating that at no time during the life of its three basic patents could their validity be questioned.

In 1945, the manufacturer stopped paying royalties due Dr. Bucky, contending that the patents were invalid. In the ensuing court case, Einstein testified that this was not even a question of infringement but a simple matter of the manufacturer's stealing Dr. Bucky's idea. Dr. Bucky won the decision, but it was reversed on appeal, probably because the case was based on a patent infringement rather than on adherence to the agreement. In the end, Dr. Bucky became disgusted with the entire affair and refused to appeal the reversal.

Throughout the years of Einstein's American residency, the Buckys and the Einsteins socialized extensively, often going back and forth between Princeton and New York and frequently vacationing together.

During these years Peter Bucky kept extensive notebooks, jotting down observations about Einstein, the man, as he knew him. In these notebooks, Bucky kept records of the many conversations he had with Einstein, many of them while driving for hours to their summer homes. Later, on the basis of his notes and Bucky's memory of his conversations, these conversations were reconstructed in the format in which they appear throughout this book.

It is these dialogues that Peter Bucky is bequeathing to us all. The following pages are set up in the following manner. An introductory chapter begins with a first-person reminiscence by Peter Bucky, followed by a conversation between Bucky and Einstein on Einstein's self-perceptions. Each following chapter is broken into two parts. The first part is a biographical vignette based on personal insights gleaned from the Buckys' experiences, while the second part is a dialogue touching upon areas broached in the first part.

The never-before-published photographs from the Buckys' personal collection capture Einstein in relaxed moments and add to the intimacy of this very personal book. Sit back, then, and let Einstein into your room. Imagine these stimulating conversations taking place across from you on the sofa and revel at the anecdotal private glimpses of this very public man. Then, after letting him into your room, you may wish forever to keep him in your heart.

ALLEN G. WEAKLAND

CHAPTER ONE

Einstein the Man

1. A Private Reminiscence

An explosion of the senses seems to surround my remembrance of the several decades during which I got to know Albert Einstein probably as intimately as did any other man on earth. I hear the somewhat out-of-tune sounds of Einstein's violin playing late at night in my father's kitchen. I smell the not unpleasant aroma of his pipe tobacco wafting through the house. I hear his naive laugh, so loud that it could be heard in every room. I hear his jolly whistling early in the morning echoing in the bathroom, as often as not extemporizing a new, instantly composed tune. I feel the breezes blowing past us through the open car in which Einstein rode as my own VIP—Very Important Passenger—in travels across the United States that added up to more than 20,000 miles. I see always the faint, almost child-like smile that exuded his ever-present warmth and kindness. I taste again the many elaborate dinners that Elsa, Einstein's second wife, prepared for us when my parents and I were invited to their Princeton home.

I feel privileged, indeed, to have had the opportunity to observe this great man at such a personal level. Being with Einstein to me was almost on the level of a supernatural experience. His appearance even heightened this impression, as his face fairly glowed with a radiance rarely seen, thanks, perhaps, to his expressive eyes.

One of the main reasons Einstein was such a pleasant person to be with, to talk with, and to live with was the fact that he never tried to show you how clever he was. An innate shyness that made him shun publicity also made him so self-effacing that he could not bear to cause added work or trouble for anyone else. But despite this shyness and modesty, Einstein was always frank. If he had an opinion, he would not hesitate to let people know it. It was not that he was tactless; it was that he didn't believe in hiding his feelings.

I recall one incident in which this frankness embarrassed his wife. Our family had been invited for dinner at the Einsteins' home in Princeton. Elsa Einstein, always a good hostess who tried to make her guests feel at home, on this occasion had prepared a lovely dinner for us, the main course of which was roast beef. When my mother saw this, she turned to Mrs. Einstein and said, "Oh, I am so sorry that you have gone to so much trouble." Mrs. Einstein charmingly smiled at my mother, saying, "Not at all, Frieda. We frequently have roast beef for dinner, so I didn't go to any special trouble." When Einstein heard this, he turned, seemingly amazed, to Elsa and asked, "Since when do we always have roast beef for dinner?"

Einstein was always fond of my mother, as she was of him. And he was especially pleased with my mother's solicitude about keeping him free of publicity whenever he was with my family.

My mother spent a good deal of time composing children's songs. (One such that she wrote used the character of Franklin Roosevelt's dog, Fala, and earned the admiration of the President himself.) Of course, no greater child ever existed than the adult Einstein. Once, in an attempt to help my mother attain some publicity for her songs, Einstein went so far as to write an affidavit in her support. The affidavit was dated 7 November 1939 and read as follows:

> I have listened to a number of Mrs. Bucky's children's songs. I consider them excellent from the artistic point of view as well as concerning the adaptation to the mentality of children. These songs deserve in my opinion the earnest consideration from publishing houses interested in this field.

It was signed: Albert Einstein.

He and my mother had one thing in common, which was that they both had medical restrictions on drinking coffee. Once, though, when the Einsteins were visiting us, my mother offered him a cup, and he gladly accepted it, but on his next visit, when my mother again offered him coffee, he refused, saying, "Oh, no, Mrs. Bucky, you know I am not allowed to have coffee."

"But Professor," my mother objected, "You had coffee last time you were here."

Einstein smiled and answered, "Yes, Mrs. Bucky. I know. But, unfortunately, the devil keeps books."

The friendship between Einstein and my mother was mirrored by Mrs. Einstein's feelings for our family. Elsa Einstein was fond of us all and was always extremely hospitable when we visited. And I remember that when my mother would go to Princeton with us, she would always take with her a selection of home-made delights.

I have a letter that documents this habit, sent to me by Elsa Einstein after one of our visits. It reads as follows:

Dear Mr. Peter:

If I were somebody who would misuse kindness, then you would be very badly off, dear Mr. Peter. But thank God, I am not quite so bad. When I am in need, then I know very well that I can count on you and that has a very quieting effect on me.

In the near future, we will come to New York more often. Would you and Thomas [my brother] and Evchen [her daughter Ilse] come out to take a walk with us in this fairy-tale-like winter landscape? I have very rarely experienced such a beautiful winter.

I greet you and all your good family heartily. Tell your dear mother that we have been subsisting the past four days on Bucky delicacies. Also the wonderful kosher sausage has been honored many times by being tasted by many friends.

Cordially, Elsa Einstein

Einstein also enjoyed my mother's cooking. In one letter to her, he wrote, "I implore you not to bring any more provisions. We are working like mad to consume the heaps of glorious things. . . . Miss Dukas has had to withdraw from the unequal struggle on account of an upset stomach."

Einstein was a mirthful person, always ready to take a joke with his hearty laugh or to give one. His sense of humor was ever-present, and even when he would criticize his own friends, he always did it with a smile and in such a humorous way that one

3

could never really be angry with him. For example, once when I visited him in Princeton with my parents, I had a discussion with them during which I raised my voice. Suddenly, he interceded and said, "Mr. Peter, oh, my, you are strict with your parents!"

Einstein's laugh was a very spontaneous one that could erupt even when other people cried. He could laugh even at things that touched him deeply.

The best thing about his humor was that it could be directed at himself as well as at others. One time when we discussed his famous theory of relativity, for instance, he told me, "If my theory is proven correct, Germany will say I am one of their greatest Germans and the French will say that I am a citizen of the world. But if it should happen that the theory is incorrect, I am sure that the French will call me a German, and the Germans will call me a Jew."

Another time, one of Einstein's young relatives made a special trip to see him in Berlin, and, finding Einstein absent, became quite upset. When Einstein heard this, he wrote him a note that read as follows: "I hear that you are dissatisfied because you did not see your Uncle Einstein. Let me, therefore, tell you what I look like: pale face, long hair, and a tiny beginning of a paunch. In addition, an awkward gait, and a cigar in the mouth (if he happens to have a cigar) and a penniless pocket. But crooked legs and warts he does not have, so he is quite handsome. It is, indeed, a pity that you did not see me."

I will always remember Einstein laughing uncontrollably when his cat became so scared at the sight of a smoked fish that he ran away at top speed.

Einstein raised simplicity to an art form in his daily grooming and dress. There were always those who criticized him for his lack of concern about such matters, and some even intimated that he affected this posture in an attempt to be different and thus draw attention to himself. Nothing could be further from the truth. Einstein detested publicity and would never do anything to attract attention. The truth is that he was an enemy of conformity in any guise, and this led him to dress not according to what was customary but in accordance with his own feelings.

As far as I know, Einstein only owned one tuxedo, and this was not a cutaway, which is more customary for formal wear. In fact, when Einstein received the Nobel Prize in Sweden, the tuxedo that he was wearing was reported to have been quite worn.

Of course, Einstein is universally known for his habit of going without socks. This was a practice that, as far as it is known, he began in Caputh, his summer residence outside of Berlin. Sometimes he even wore sandals without socks while attending lectures in the Institute. I often think that Einstein would have felt at home with the campus style of dress that came into vogue in the late 1960's. On the other hand, he might well have viewed it as a new form of conformity.

An incident that typified Einstein's approach to dress occurred in 1925 in the Tiergarten in Berlin. Einstein was walking with a young lady student in the park after a heavy rain. Puddles dotted the entire area, and Einstein carefully stepped around them. Finally, he confessed to the girl why he was taking this circuitous route: his shoes had several holes in them. Since it was unthinkable for him to have these shoes resoled unless they were nearly falling apart, his only alternative was to tread cautiously.

This also reminds me of a time when I was driving Einstein to a summer home in Old Lyme, Connecticut. We were riding in a convertible with the top down, as Einstein loved to feel the wind blowing through his curly hair. But this happened to be a rare occasion, as Einstein was wearing a felt hat. All of a sudden, a heavy downpour commenced so quickly that I didn't have time to get the top back up. Einstein immediately took off the hat and tucked it under his coat. Noticing that I was surprised by this action, he smiled and said, "Herr Peter, you see, my hair has withstood water many times before, but I don't know how many times my felt hat can withstand it."

Einstein in an open car could often provoke some unusual responses. Once, while he was visiting our family in New York, I took him for a ride through the Bronx in our convertible. His famous long hair was blowing in the wind as we breezed through the city streets, and as we passed a cluster of people on the sidewalk, one woman suddenly shouted to the others, "Oh, look, there goes Mahatma Gandhi!"

Driving the professor around was always an adventure, not only for the conversations we enjoyed but also for the amusing inci-

5

dents that always seemed to happen. Once, for instance, Einstein was scheduled to lecture in Princeton, and I was driving him there from New York. On the New Jersey Turnpike, I began speeding to accommodate Einstein, who was anxious lest we be late. Seeing lights behind us, Einstein turned to me and asked, "Ist der boese feind da," which translated meant, "Is the bad enemy coming?" ("The bad enemy" was Einstein's favorite pet name for the police.) Sure enough, a New Jersey State Trooper pulled us over. But as soon as the trooper looked in the car and saw Einstein, he exclaimed, embarrassedly, "Oh, I beg your pardon, I didn't know that you had the German ambassador in your car." Apparently, the trooper knew that he had seen that face in the newspapers with some connection to Germany. Even though we were let off the hook, Einstein felt insulted that he had been called a German when he, in fact, had had to flee Germany's Nazis.

Even in a car on the open road, it was difficult for Einstein to hide from the limelight. On another occasion when I was driving him on the New Jersey Turnpike, I spotted a State Trooper in my rear-view mirror approaching us on a motorcycle. This time, I knew that I wasn't speeding. Einstein again asked, "What does the bad enemy want—you didn't do anything wrong?"

The mystery ended when the trooper pulled us over and came to the car, asking, "Are you Professor Einstein?" When Einstein nodded, the trooper said, "I'm sorry, Professor, to have stopped you, but there is an urgent telephone call for you from New York." He then escorted us to the nearest telephone booth and rang the New York number. It was a scenario that might have been lifted from the pages of George Orwell's *1984*.

Einstein loved sitting next to the driver in a car and would have detested the proliferation of limousines that we see today all over the streets of major cities. He would often say to me while we drove, "What a waste of energy actually is the modern automobile." Then he would go into a long lecture explaining that approximately 1/300th of the power used in an automobile—that is, one horsepower—could get you to the same place, albeit a bit more slowly. He attributed the wasted power to the egos of men and to boys who enjoyed impressing girlfriends with jackrabbit starts and screeching tires.

Another incident involving Einstein's "bad enemy" occurred one summer when, on a hot day, we decided to drive from Princeton to the lovely New Jersey shore community of Spring Lake, which is known by some locals as the Irish Riviera. We decided to find an isolated section of the beach to lie on and enjoy the sea breezes. Unfortunately, at the time the community required a pass for its private beaches. It wasn't long before a Spring Lake policeman showed up and ordered us off the beach. Some famous people would have taken umbrage at this, implying that their fame placed them above the petty laws of the commoners. But not Einstein. He modestly rose and complied with the policeman's order. But I have often wondered if that dutiful policeman ever realized that he had evicted one of the greatest men of our times.

Einstein's wife, Elsa, always nagged him about his habits of dress. Once when she was scolding him I heard Einstein offer the rejoinder: "It would be a sad thing if the bag was better than the meat which is wrapped in it!"

Einstein's dress was, I think, simply an extension of his philosophy, which sought to reduce everything personal to its simplest level. Not wearing socks, for instance, eliminated the need for anyone ever to darn them.

Similarly, wearing his hair longer helped him avoid wasting time at the barber shop. Indeed, once I even asked him why he didn't use lather on his face when he shaved, and he replied, "Well, I can shave just as well with plain water."

So great was his disregard for normal practices and commonly accepted etiquette that one of the books that Einstein found most amusing was an Emily Post book of etiquette. I will never forget the times when Einstein, while staying with us in New York, would retire to his study late at night. Invariably, when we heard loud laughter resounding through the house and ran upstairs to check, we would find him with this Emily Post book out, thoroughly amused. Often he would share with us whatever section of the book he considered outlandishly funny.

Einstein used to let himself in for some severe reprimands from Elsa because of his habit of returning from trips with the luggage that she had carefully packed for him missing articles of clothing that he had either lost or forgotten. Once, after a stern warning from Elsa to be more careful, she was amazed to find upon his return that his trunk was perfectly packed, with nothing missing. When Elsa asked him who had packed for him, he said, smiling, "Nobody." Later he confessed that, upon arrival at his destination, he had simply gone to the nearest store and bought a new shirt so that he would not be bothered with repacking. What he didn't notice was that the neck of the shirt was two sizes too large.

It was impossible to persuade Einstein to go to a store to buy a new suit. Whenever attempts were made to get Einstein to go to a tailor, he would grumble, "This is not necessary. My old suit is still good enough and I don't need a new one." Mrs. Einstein would solve this problem by taking one of his old suits to a tailor and having a new one made according to its measurements.

At any rate, he would prefer to wear a pullover rather than a suit. And he was the same with casual wear as he was with suits. He preferred sitting around in a robe with holes in it to wearing a new one.

Once, when I was feeling particularly bold, I suggested that perhaps the time had come for him to get a new sweater. When I was greeted with a stony silence, I retreated, realizing that I had infringed upon holy territory, and I never again ventured such a comment.

One of the most fitting comments Einstein ever made concerning dress was in a note written to a twelve-year-old boy who had sent him a set of cuff links and a necktie as a gift. In thanking the boy, Einstein wrote: "Your gift will be an appropriate suggestion to be a little more elegant in the future than hitherto, because neckties and cuffs existed for me only as a remote memory."

Einstein's logic sometimes extended into solving daily problems via the scientific method. Once, for instance, he was invited to attend an official dinner in New York, where his host provided for a four-room suite at the Waldorf-Astoria. In the evening when it came time for Einstein to dress in his formal attire, he discovered that he had lost a collar button. After a search, he remarked, "From now on, I will only live in one of the four rooms and close the other three, so that if in the future I am missing something, I only have to look for it in one room instead of in four." Einstein had developed a fool-proof theory for finding lost buttons with only one-fourth of the effort.

One of Einstein's most enchanting qualities was a certain naivete, rarely found in great men. This was demonstrated often in his enjoyment of puzzles and tricks. Often he would spend weeks trying to analyze their functions. I will never forget one occasion when I bought him one of those drinking birds that would alternately dip its head into a glass of water and then raise it. Einstein was so intrigued by this that he spent about three and one-half months figuring out that the process was caused by evaporation when he could have easily discovered this simply by scratching the glass bird's paint off. Although I had suggested this to him in the beginning, he refused, insisting on solving the problem intuitively.

The universality of Einstein's knowledge always amazed me, and, except for that drinking bird, he showed a rare ability to quickly grasp the basic ideas of a wide variety of subjects. Often, my father would ask for assistance in solving some technical problem. Einstein would try to solve it right away, and he often succeeded. At other times, he would work late into the night, but he would never fail next morning to write my father a letter with the answer.

In the backyard of my family's residence at 5 East 76th Street in Manhattan, my father had a development shop where he employed a mechanic and a physicist who developed his ideas for products that were later manufactured. Einstein loved to go to this shop, where he would often engage in heated discussions with those assistants. And input during those discussions was often beneficial.

Einstein never let his ego get in the way of the truth. I remember many times when he would argue for hours about theories in physics arising from my father's experiments. After a few days, Einstein would charge down the stairs from his office and laughingly say to my father, "Bucky, you were right, after all! I have made a mistake." He would say this with such a hearty, open, child-like laugh that I really felt that he was happy about discovering his error.

Being in the presence of Einstein and my father was an education in the application of the scientific method. They could discuss scientific principles and inventions for hours. My mother has written that after visits to our home, Einstein would leave, taking along the unsolved problems.

"And at night he usually wrote long letters to my husband, adding to them in the morning," she said. "The problems were sometimes solved."

Einstein could also be quite comical. Once, after trying to use one of my father's inventions, he wrote saying, "Trembling, I take up my pen." He then went on to describe how the machine had failed to work for him and suggested that a refrigerator on the same circuit might have caused the malfunction. But he said it was much more likely that the machine was suffering from the "Pauli Effect," symptoms of which Einstein had diagnosed in himself on several occasions. He went on to explain that for years a certain Wolfgang Pauli had had the effect of putting physical apparatuses and household appliances out of order simply by being near them. He compared this to a mischievous cook's poisoning his diners with cyanide: he decides to do the job up right by using double the quantity, but then ends up only able to kill half the number of people. He then pleaded with my father: "Don't be angry with me on account of the Pauli Effect."

Einstein would never accept any preferential treatment. Even though, for instance, he was offered honorary citizenship of the United States after only three weeks in the country, he insisted on waiting five years like everyone else. This attitude was so ingrained and so well-known to his intimates that his personal assistant, Helen Dukas, once had a dream demonstrating the point. In the dream, robbers broke into Einstein's house and required everyone to stand against the wall and surrender their valuables. When they reached Einstein they said that from him they could take nothing. But Einstein became enraged at this "affront" and reached into his pocket to give the robbers a ten-cent piece, which was all that he carried on his person.

Einstein and I often talked about the problems of power in the world. He detested any displays of chauvinism or power. The only power that impressed him was that of nature. On occasions when he happened upon a street parade, he would turn his back and leave. Once, in fact, he remarked, "If I see anybody marching with joy to music, then already I have something against this man. He has received his big brain by mistake, and a spine could have been enough for him."

Einstein had a remarkable consideration for other people, especially for those less fortunate than he. I recall his sister, Maja, telling me of an occasion when Einstein was staying in Switzerland. At the time, he was boarding in a house the owner of which prepared his meals for him. One day, when Maja was visiting him and coffee was served, Einstein begged his sister to drink out of the same cup as he, so that the landlady would not have to wash two cups.

Another time, when we were driving to New London, Connecticut, on our way to our summer home in Watch Hill, Rhode Island, I was discussing with Einstein the fact that he always seemed to favor the person he considered an underdog. Einstein smiled and said, "Yes, I believe this is true. I speak to everyone in the same way whether he is a garbage man or the president of a university."

This modesty and unpretentiousness never seemed to change. People who didn't know him sometimes found it hard to believe that the great Einstein could be so unaware of his status, and they would presume that his unpretentiousness was all artifice. For instance, once while we were visiting him in Princeton, we all decided to go out to a movie. Einstein bought all of our tickets, but when we went into the theater we were told that it would be another fifteen or twenty minutes before the movie started.

Of course, it was anathema for Einstein to sit anywhere for that long without anything to do, so he suggested that we take a short walk. As we passed the ticket collector, Einstein turned to him with concern and asked, "Will you recognize us when we come back in again without giving up our tickets?" The ticket collector thought that this was a joke, but he didn't know Einstein, who would never assume that anyone would recognize him. At any rate, we joked about this as we walked and window-shopped in downtown Princeton.

A little-known fact about Einstein is that he was the first living person to have his bust carved in one of the panels in the Riverside Church in New York City. Characteristically, he told me that he was not at all impressed by the honor. But he was particularly amused by the fact that this honor was bestowed upon him—a Jew—by a Christian church.

The one essential in keeping Einstein as a friend was that one always had to be truthful. If he ever discovered that someone had been less than truthful with him he would never again have faith in that person. Although his native civility would dissuade him from holding a grudge, he would act thereafter with a great deal of reservation.

It was satisfying to the spirit to see how trusting Einstein could be of our family. We helped protect him from publicity and he, in turn, rewarded us with the utmost loyalty. I recall once when David Sarnoff, the top executive of one of the nation's largest electronic concerns, Radio Corporation of America, approached my father with the idea that Einstein and my father should join RCA's newest research division. Since Sarnoff had no prior contact with Einstein, my father arranged for a meeting in Old Lyme.

Present at the meeting were Einstein, my father, Helen Dukas, my mother, and myself. In the middle of the meeting, my father received an urgent telephone call from one of his patients and excused himself. While he was out of the room, Sarnoff arose from his chair, walked over to where Einstein was sitting, and whispered something in his ear. Einstein immediately stood and announced, "Mr. Sarnoff, I am not interested in the proposition." He then marched out of the room. Surprised, we all got up and followed him, curious as to what Sarnoff had said. Later, he told us that Sarnoff had whispered, "Professor, truthfully, we only want you. We don't want Dr. Bucky in this set-up."

Thus, Einstein pre-dated by some three decades, the spirit of Tom Paxton's folk-song "Ramblin' Boy":

> In Tulsa town, we chanced to stray.
> We thought we'd try to work one day.
> The boss said that he had room for one;
> Said my old pal, "We'd rather bum."

Another example of Einstein's faithfulness to my father occurred before World War II. In 1929, while we were living in Germany, my father was called to Berlin to take the post of director of the

X-ray department of the Rudolf Virchow Hospital. At the time, one of the directors of that hospital was a man named Lichtwitz. My father formed a friendship with Professor Lichtwitz and at some point introduced him to Einstein.

When my father returned to the United States in 1933, he obtained a position for Professor Lichtwitz as a leading physician at Montefiore Hospital in New York. Soon after that, Professor Lichtwitz was placed in charge of an important conference at the hospital and, calling upon his introduction to Einstein, invited the physicist to the conference.

Shortly before the conference was to take place, Einstein learned that Lichtwitz had not invited my father, to whom he owed his position. As soon as he learned of this, Einstein wrote the following letter:

Dear Professor Lichtwitz:

Accidentally, I was informed today that Doctor Bucky has not been invited to the occasion this coming Thursday. I must assume that this action is a very serious slight against my dearest living friend who, on account of his extraordinary achievements in the field of medicine and who had an unending friendship towards me no matter what the price, is much more entitled to receive an invitation than myself. I am so hurt by this action that it is completely impossible for me to attend the meeting this coming Thursday. Of course, Dr. Bucky knows nothing of this letter, nor does he know that I will not attend this meeting. Please be informed, also, that sending Dr. Bucky an invitation at this late date will be of no value in reversing my decision. I personally will write the director of this occasion to apologize for not attending. With friendly greetings,

Yours,
Albert Einstein

Einstein always appeared to be in control of himself emotionally. I never saw him lose his temper. Nor did I ever see him indulge in any sentimentality, save for two occasions. One of these was when his wife, Elsa, died. I had never seen him shed a tear, but he did then as he sighed, "Oh, I shall really miss her." The other occasion was when he wrote to my father following a particularly difficult surgery that my father had undergone. "From now on," he wrote, "I will be thankful for every hour of my life that we are left together."

On the other hand, he could be gracious in demonstrating his friendship. I carry a picture in my mind of him in Princeton, walking out to the car with us when it was time to leave and standing there until we drove away. There he would be, waving to us as the car moved slowly down Mercer Street.

But most of all I recall the glorious summers. That most special time when it came to socializing with Einstein. For it was then that our families invariably got together, often to relax in our summer vacation spots: Watch Hill, Rhode Island; Saranac Lake, New York; Old Lyme, Connecticut, and Nassau Point, Long Island. All settings for lazy summer days when I got to know the *real* Einstein at his leisure.

There were two primary conditions to be met in selecting a summer vacation spot. First and foremost for Einstein was the question: "How are sailing conditions?" For this was the professor's consuming leisure passion. The second requirement was that the summer home be isolated from population and, especially, from commercialism. Our four spots met both of those conditions perfectly and were, to Einstein, little corners of paradise on earth.

Watch Hill, Rhode Island, was one of our favorites. Situated near Newport, next to the clothing-mill center of Westerly, Watch Hill had no hotel and no commercial establishment, except two food shops, a shoemaker, a locksmith, and a hardware store.

The house we rented was called "The Studio" and was on the top of a mountain overlooking the water. While we were there in the summer of 1934 Einstein tried to keep up with world news, particularly about the newest activities of the Nazis. The only authentic news of them that we could receive speedily came directly from Germany via short-wave radio. Unfortunately, at that time short-wave transmission was still in its infancy and reception in Watch Hill was problematic.

Always being one to tinker with inventions and gadgets (a streak inherited from my father, no doubt), I resolved to improve matters by building our own huge short-wave receiving station, which worked very well and enabled Einstein to listen to a continuous flow of news from his homeland. After that summer, Einstein gave me a picture of himself, which he inscribed in German. "For the technical amusement director, Peter, during our stay in Watch Hill, 1934."

Another of Einstein's most enjoyable vacations was at Saranac Lake. One of the reasons Einstein loved this place so much was that it was very wooded, compared with our other vacation spots, which all tended to open lakes and beaches. The trees and forests appealed to his love of nature. I can picture him still, walking in the woods for hours, contentedly observing every weed, insect, and flower.

Once, while walking together in these woods, we noticed a common earthworm. I questioned Einstein about how it could be that one could cut a worm in two and have both halves take on lives of their own. Einstein's response, rather than dispelling the mystery, displayed his simple wonder at nature's marvels. "You see," he said, "this is nature. Nature has many puzzles and marvels and there are many things that we do not understand yet about nature. This is why my religion is really the universe—in other words, nature, which is our reflection of the universe."

During our Saranac Lake vacation, Einstein became friendly with the Bloomingdales, who had a summer home there. Despite their great wealth (The brothers Lyman and Joseph Bloomingdale were the founders in 1872 of the famous department store that bears their name), the Bloomingdales were relatively simple people, a fact that attracted Einstein to them.

On several occasions, Einstein was even induced to join us in visits to Florida, although this took the greatest of efforts as Einstein had an image of Florida as luxury, and a snobbish one, at that. But his friendship with my father always won out, since my father required the benefits of the Florida climate for recuperative purposes after difficult surgery for an intestinal blockage.

During our vacation time, the routine rarely varied. It was a congenial atmosphere where everyone was at ease and watches or clocks were only a memory. After breakfast in the morning, Einstein liked to read the newspapers, after which discussions would ensue on the latest news. Then my father and he would usually go for a long walk. My father enjoyed these walks with Einstein very much, and they were fruitful hours when the two developed new thoughts and ideas.

We spent one very nice summer together in Old Lyme. Oddly enough, the house that we stayed in was called the Little White House, as it resembled in outer appearance the White House in Washington, where Einstein had once, in 1934, spent the night as the guest of Franklin Roosevelt. The country is beautiful in that part of Connecticut, and there was plenty of time and space for Einstein to sail. In this regard, Old Lyme was particularly enjoyable for Einstein as the town had been a center for sailboat-building for generations. He enjoyed hanging around some of the town folk, watching the builders ply their trade, swapping sailing stories and getting advice from the experts. Einstein had his favorite sailboat, a modest catboat, transported everywhere he went for vacation.

It was curious that Einstein should have chosen sailing as a hobby because he couldn't swim a stroke. In those days, many of us at the Watch Hill summer home would use the ocean as a natural bath. Einstein preferred the safety of a bathtub. Once, though, while he was sailing in Watch Hill, a strong gust of wind overturned his sailboat. Einstein, clinging for his life to the side of the sailboat while clinging as well to his sense of humor, said to his companion, "This bath must be counted to my credit."

Einstein's love for sailing precluded any mechanical interference such as outboard motors or auxiliary engines. He believed that the essence of sailing was total independence from artificial propulsion. Sometimes he carried this belief to extremes, to the great anxiety of his friends. Once at Watch Hill, for example, we all waited with growing concern for his return from an afternoon sail. Finally, at 11:00 P.M., we decided to send the Coast Guard out to search for him. The guardsmen found him out in the bay, not in the least concerned about his situation, confident that the wind would eventually return him to Watch Hill.

Einstein's step-daughter Margot and others often spoke in romantic terms of his sailing. "Going on the boat meant to him that he was together with the elements," she once said. "And when you were with him on the boat you felt him as an element. He had something so natural and strong in him because he was himself a piece of nature. He sailed like Odysseus." Local sailors in areas where we vacationed, however, sometimes indicated that Einstein's sailing skills were suspect.

One eyewitness from our Peconic Bay summers was quoted recently as saying, "He wasn't a natural sailor. It didn't come easy for him. I remember reminding him innumerable times that you should duck when you are going about, so the boom wouldn't hit him."

"Various members of the club used to try to help him," the eyewitness recalled. "Frequently he would get becalmed out in the bay, and we would pull him out with our rowboats. He certainly had a lot of perseverance. Frequently he would go out all day long, just drifting around. He apparently was just out there meditating."

But despite naysaying such as this, I believe that Einstein was more skillful than he is given credit for. For example, one of his sailing friends, the biochemist Leon Watters, who visited us in Peconic once, wrote: "Once when out sailing with him, and while we were engaged in an interesting conversation, I suddenly cried out, 'Achtung!' For we were almost upon another boat. He veered away with excellent control and when I remarked what a close call we had had, he started to laugh and sailed directly toward one boat after another, much to my horror; but he always veered off in time and then laughed like a naughty boy."

I think, rather, that Einstein's drifting and getting stuck in calm waters was simply a sign of his own desire to use sailing as another way of finding the serenity that might enable him to theorize more efficiently. To the average person, after all, being becalmed for hours might be a terrible trial. To Einstein, this could simply have provided more free time to think.

Once, in fact, a good friend gave him an expensive outboard motor for emergencies. Einstein, without any discussion, had it returned immediately.

Actually, Einstein could be quite cavalier about his safety. And he craved sailing so much that he would even ignore bad weather. I recall one day when he insisted on going out on his catboat in a thunderstorm. Our family argued, pleaded, and cajoled, but to no avail. He tried to explain that the chance of lightning striking such a small target as his sailboat was infinitesimal. The top of his mast, he said, was far too low for the lightning to strike, as there would surely be taller objects to attract the electrical charge. Holding our breath, we wondered who else would have a taller object out on the lake in such weather.

Einstein devoted most of his vacation afternoons to sailing, though my father did most of the work. Einstein would sit next to the rudder, steering the boat, occasionally, to his embarrassment, striking a rock. Any of his guests invited aboard were usually given the honor of raising the sails, pushing off, and performing the other menial chores of sailing. His sailboat, despite his great stature, was small and quite primitive. There were never enough seats for all of the guests, so people often had to sit on the deck.

My father has been quoted as saying, "The natural counterplay of wind and water delighted him most. Speed, records, and, above all, competition were against his nature. He had a child-like delight when there was a calm and the boat came to a standstill, or when the boat ran aground."

Einstein would brook no luxuries. Primitivity was the essence of sailing, in his opinion. This often had disastrous consequences for others, including my father, who more than once came home with a sore bottom from sitting for hours on the boat's hardwood deck. My father complained about his stubbornness until Einstein finally relented and allowed him to bring a pillow aboard. (Actually, my father had a double purpose in getting a pillow on board, for it could also serve as a life preserver, something Einstein had never allowed).

A footnote to Einstein's sailing adventures: One of our summer vacation spots figured in the history of the twentieth century. At Peconic Bay, Long Island, a vacation was interrupted by a pilgrimage of physicists who came to warn Einstein of developments in Germany that were threatening to lead to Hitler's getting an atomic weapon. But I will return to this summer surprise later.

Despite the fact that Einstein did not like to appear in public and hated to be in the limelight, he would still go all out to do a favor for his friends. Once, for example, against our advice, he suddenly appeared at one of our family's large wedding parties, which was held at New York's Plaza Hotel. He showed up wearing a knitted cap, a plain suit, and—most unusual for him—a tie. His presence caused so much excitement that, to protect his privacy, we had to transfer him to the bridal suite upstairs.

Even when publicity precautions failed, Einstein could still be quite gracious. I recall once when my brother was sick in the Bronx Veterans Hospital and Einstein decided to pay a visit. Word got out, and by the time Einstein arrived a sizable crowd had gathered. Among those waiting for him was the hospital rabbi who was anxious to meet him. When he arrived and shook the rabbi's hand, the rabbi apologized profusely, saying that he had no right to impose upon Einstein's privacy. Einstein stopped the apology, saying, "Oh, no, you have the right because, after all, you work for a very important boss."

It amazed me to what lengths people would go for an opportunity to meet Einstein. Many schemes that played on his well-known good-heartedness were hatched even by people who were famous in their own right. For example, Eartha Kitt, determined to meet the professor but realizing how many hurdles she would have to jump to see him, finally offered to contribute several thousand dollars to his favorite charity as an inducement. But Einstein held to his refusal to be an object of adoration.

Einstein was not averse to wealth, per se. He had quite a number of wealthy friends. But his first requirement was that a person had to have a sincere desire for his friendship rather than for publicity.

One of his wealthy friends was Dr. Leon Watters, who was president of the Watters Medical Supply Company in New York. Another was the owner of the Breyers Ice Cream Company, whom Einstein met during a ferry boat ride that we took between Manhattan and New Jersey. At one point, the conversation turned to ice cream and Einstein's love for it. After that, every month for the rest of his life, Einstein received a gift of twenty-five quarts of Breyers Ice Cream.

But Einstein deeply resented invitations from so-called friends given as subterfuges to enable them to show him off to other friends. And it wasn't easy to fool Einstein with this sort of charade.

An amusing incident occurred once when I went to see him off on a flight from Newark Airport. It was in the heyday of the gossip

19

columnist Walter Winchell. Winchell had somehow got wind of Einstein's plans and he sent one of his spies to the airport to snoop around. The fellow asked us all sorts of questions, but I told him nothing. He managed only to get my name from me, but of course he recognized Einstein.

Traveling with Einstein was also his sister, Maja, and his secretary, Helen Dukas. Winchell's man learned somehow that Maja was Einstein's sister, but he was unable to identify Miss Dukas. Consequently, in his gossip column the next day, Winchell reported that Einstein had been at Newark Airport with his sister, Maja, along with "Mr. and Mrs. Peter A. Bucky." The account generated a lot of congratulatory telephone calls from friends who knew me as a bachelor.

As long as I knew Einstein, he was hounded by this problem of publicity. On another occasion, also at Newark Airport, Einstein had traveled from Princeton to Manhattan to visit our family, as he did about every two weeks, usually for a two- or three-day stay. (Often, during these stays, we would take him out for a Broadway play, which meant ushering him in through side doors of the theaters.) On this occasion, as I drove Einstein back to Princeton, we passed Newark Airport off of Route 1. Einstein suddenly became filled with boyish enthusiasm over the airport and wanted to explore the place.

Within a few minutes of our arrival, the place was abuzz with rumors of his presence. Soon, the Mayor of Newark showed up and wanted to welcome the scientist to New Jersey's largest city. Einstein graciously, but with some embarrassment, accepted.

His dislike of publicity often came in conflict with his natural instinct to be kind. For instance, it was difficult for him to refuse to sign autographs, even though he hated the practice, and he would often look desperately to his friends for help. Once, in New London, Connecticut, while we were on the way with our family to Watch Hill our car ran into mechanical troubles, and we had to stop for repairs. As usual, it didn't take long for word to spread about Einstein's presence.

Out of nowhere, a swarm of teenagers appeared bearing pens and paper, seeking Einstein's autograph. Feeling set upon, he turned to me with a pleading gesture. Thinking quickly, I told him, "Just sign somebody else's name for the first person." He did, and to our astonishment the entire pack of teenagers, grumbling, went on their way.

Another time, under similar circumstances, I suggested that he should write his name smaller and smaller on each autograph until it finally would be too small to read. This also succeeded in dispersing the crowd.

Some people, though, were very determined. Once, as we walked up the long steps to the New York Public Library, a well-dressed woman approached and exclaimed, "Oh, are you not Professor Einstein?" Distressed, the professor muttered, "I'm sorry, but you must be mistaken." As we walked into the library, we became aware that the same woman was following us doggedly. We had been in the library for about a half-hour when the same woman confronted Einstein again and said loudly, "Und sie sind es doch!" which in German means, "And it is you!" All we could do was laugh.

On the other hand, if Einstein did not feel threatened by a public situation that might degenerate into a circus of adulation or autograph-seeking, the results could be both charming and amusing. For instance, the professor told me that he once found himself at a public function sitting next to a teenager who, refreshingly for Einstein, did not recognize the celebrity at his side. Einstein engaged the boy in conversation, and after a while the boy asked him, "What do you do for a living?" Einstein replied, "The study of physics." Seemingly shocked, the boy responded, "What! At your age? I finished that two years ago!" In telling the story, Einstein remarked on how much he admired this naiveté and frankness in children.

This story is similar to another one that Einstein related to our family while we were vacationing in Peconic Bay. Einstein was laughing as he returned from a walk, and when we asked what was so funny, he told us of meeting a boy about ten years of age. The boy had asked, "Excuse me, you're Mr. Einstein?" When Einstein confirmed that he was, the boy, who was accompanied by his mother, had said, "Would you mind if I had my picture taken with you, because mathematics is my worst subject." Einstein, of course, allowed the boy's mother to snap a picture of them together. I often wondered whether any of Einstein's mathematical wizardry rubbed off on the boy.

Also, Einstein had a genuine desire to mingle with common people and would occasionally give free rein to that desire by accompanying my mother on grocery-shopping forays. While roaming the aisles of the store, he would show his simplicity, chiding my mother, for instance, for buying apples when she had already bought pears.

Einstein was so publicity-shy and modest that he even shied away from important symbolic gestures offered to honor him, such as the naming of scientific buildings, schools, or hospitals after him. One particular struggle in this vein began when the president of Yeshiva College approached him with the idea of building a medical school bearing Einstein's name. Einstein demurred, saying that since he had never accomplished anything in the field of medicine, there was no justification for thus honoring him. Only after many of his closest friends, including my father, convinced him that the medical school would allow many more young Jewish boys to pursue medical careers did Einstein allow the use of his name for the school, which still stands in New York as a tribute to Einstein.

Of course, it would be easy to attribute his dislike of publicity to snobbishness, but nothing could be further from the truth. It stemmed both from his genuine modesty and from an instinct to fend off people seeking to take advantage of him or his name.

One Sunday, for instance, when Einstein was staying with us in New York, we took him for a long drive in the suburbs. That night, we were very tired. But just as we were looking forward to a quiet evening at home, the telephone rang. Somehow, Dr. Allan Dafoe, a Canadian physician who had gained notoriety by delivering a set of quintuplets in Canada, had learned that Einstein was staying with us. Dr. Dafoe said he just happened to be in town, along with the nurse who had assisted him in the quintuplets' delivery, and wondered if they could come over to talk for a few minutes. At first, Einstein declined, but as Dr. Dafoe persisted he finally gave in.

Within a half-hour, Dr. Dafoe and his nurse arrived, promising that there would be no publicity. His few minutes turned into an hour. When he left, we all said we had found him unimpressive. We agreed that he was probably just a country doctor who had happened to be in the right place at the right time. We gave the matter no more thought that night.

But next morning, to our astonishment, almost all of New York's newspapers reported that the great Einstein had met with the famous Dr. Dafoe. Wondering how the papers could have learned of the meeting, I did a little investigating. To my disgust, and the professor's, I learned that the "nurse" that Dafoe had brought along for the meeting was no nurse, at all, but a representative of United Press International. This story underscores the prudence of Einstein in avoiding publicity. The doctor was seeking, after all, only to further his own career.

For many years, Einstein's physicians attempted to persuade him to stop smoking his pipe. My father, in a friendly manner, also tried to influence him to at least reduce the habit. In fact, my father, a pioneer in X-ray technology, would often X-ray Einstein, a procedure to which he submitted with intense interest. For a while, Helen Dukas would only give him one pipe to smoke every Sunday. He tried hard to follow this rule because he was convinced of the dangers of smoking, and he tried especially in the presence of my father. And whenever my father noticed that he was smoking, Einstein would affect a schoolboyish air of shame.

After Einstein's wife died, he went through a terrible period of stomach problems. My father tried to find ways to ease his discomfort and once devised a special diet for him. Though usually cavalier about medical advice, Einstein was appreciative and wrote to my father, saying, "I am grateful . . . and now feel sincere respect both for you and for your so pertinent art in general. If there would be any relapse whatsoever on my part, please refer back to this declaration."

All of these things represented Einstein the man to me. And everything—his daily way of life, his play, his work, his words— harmonized, a miraculous accomplishment in an increasingly discordant world. In this sense, I don't think that Einstein belonged spiritually to this century.

But I, for one, am glad that he lived in *my* century and that I had the privilege of counting myself as one of those few intimates to whom he opened his soul. During the several decades in which he graced my life, and especially during those many occasions when he and I drove thousands of miles together, the opportunity developed to converse with this great man on numerous subjects and at great length.

The anecdotes and conversations throughout this book stem from my reminiscences of that thirty-year span during which I knew Einstein both in Germany and in the United States. I offer them to posterity in the hope that the world might come to love and admire him as much as I did—and still do.

2. Conversation: Einstein's Self-Perceptions

BUCKY: When was it that you knew that you wanted to make physics your life's work?

EINSTEIN: When I moved to Aarau, Switzerland, in 1896 and was attending the ETH [Eidgenossische Technische Hochschule], for the first time I realized how set I was against the drilling and memorizing of formulas that was involved in mathematics. It was then, I suppose, that I took an intense interest in physics.

BUCKY: Did you not feel that, despite your hatred of drilling involved in mathematics, you might need that discipline for your work in physics?

EINSTEIN: Well, at a very early age, I made an assumption, which was that a successful physicist only needs to know elementary mathematics, which he needs for the application of the development of a series of formulae, and that all the rest of mathematics is completely unfruitful as the tools of the average processes that a physicist uses. At a later time, with great regret, I realized that the assumption of mine was completely wrong.

BUCKY: Did this regret concerning this lack of interest in mathematics severely hamper your work in later years?

EINSTEIN: In some ways, yes, but on the other hand, even after I became well-known I many times made use of experts to assist me in complicated calculations in order to prove certain physics problems. Also, I have always strongly believed that one should not burden his mind with formulae when he can go to a textbook and look them up. I have done that, too, on many occasions. I still feel that, if one gets too involved with higher mathematics, one uses too much energy that can be more beneficially applied to the main goal at hand.

BUCKY: Did you have any affinity for any subjects other than physics?

EINSTEIN: I was very single-minded in my interests as a student. I recall, for example, being called into the office of a Professor Pernet, one of my graduate teachers. He said to me, "Einstein, I have called you into my office because I wanted you to understand that physics, itself, is not an easy subject to study. I know that you are very conscientious and you certainly have good will, but your results do not show it. If I may make a suggestion without hurting your feelings, it might be a better idea if you took some other subjects like medicine or, perhaps, even if you studied to become a lawyer."

I answered him, "For those subjects, Professor, I have no understanding at all and I would prefer physics. I feel that I should at least try and see how I get along with physics." No, I never cared much for other subjects. I failed at botany, zoology, and French, and often this would cause me to fail the entire curriculum. Perhaps the only other subject that I really cared for was literature. I had one particular professor who was responsible for awakening this interest in literature and I, perhaps wrongly, assumed that he noticed the fact that my interest was aroused. This professor lived in Munich, and one time, after I had been appointed a professor myself, I had a strange desire to call on him. But I was amazed to discover that he did not recognize me at all, and on top of that, he considered my visit to be peculiar. I think in retrospect that he was suspicious that I had visited him in order to borrow money from him.

For some reason, this made me realize that I was on my own, so to speak—fully independent in respect to everybody—and I felt after that that I owed no obligation to any individual.

BUCKY: Are some of those stories true about your great difficulties in school, or are they simply legend?

25

EINSTEIN: Oh, yes, they are quite true. I remember in Munich having my Latin teacher tell me that I would never be able to do anything that would make sense in this life. Fortunately, I was very determined to do what I intended to do, but my abilities were very modest, and I had to understand everything through my own handiwork.

I was always very anxious to get a better understanding of things. In fact, once I got a bawling out from an elementary school teacher who told me, "Einstein, you must stop asking me so many questions. You know I do not have answers for some of them. What will the other students think of this?"

But as a student, it was quite difficult for me to grasp some of the basic theories because I had an extremely bad memory. I knew for this reason that my future studies would not be an easy task. When I took the entrance examinations for the engineering division, I realized with great pain how incomplete my previous schooling had been. I failed that exam—which was completely just. But thanks to the kindness of a couple of people—the physicist [Heinrich] Weber and Prof. Albin Herzos—I was able to go to the Kantonschule in Aarau.

BUCKY: So we come full circle to where physics became your major interest.

EINSTEIN: Yes, exactly. It was in Aarau, actually, that I made my first, rather primitive, experiments in thinking that had a direct bearing on the Special Theory [of Relativity]. The thought that I had at that time was that if a person could run after a light wave with the same speed as light, you would have a wave arrangement which could be completely independent of time. Of course, such a thing is impossible, but invention is not the result of any logical thinking even if the end product is directly tied to the logical figuration. Even after I passed the exam for the ETH, I was resigned to being just an average student. To be a good student, one must be able to grasp the new things that you learn quickly. Also, one must be willing with all of his might to concentrate on that which is being taught. Also, one must have an orderly and systematic way of putting down in writing everything that you hear in class so that one can develop it further. Most of these disciplines I did not possess, regretfully. I learned to face this with an inner peace. All that I cared about was filling myself with more knowledge.

BUCKY: How did you overcome these disadvantages?

EINSTEIN: Well, I used my own time at home to great advantage. Often, if I was not interested in a particular lecture, I played hookey and studied much more theoretical physics at home than I would have gotten in school. I felt that this was a good idea, and it also eased my bad conscience and enabled me to maintain my equilibrium. Also, I had developed at this school a deep friendship with one of the other students, named Marcel Grossman. Every week, we went to a cafe called "The Metropole," which was located near the Limmajquai, where we discussed not only our studies but mostly other things which all young people are interested in and into which they look with open eyes. He was not a vagabond or a loner like I was, but a man who was very closely tied to the Swiss way of life.

But he had a strong inner independence, nevertheless. He had one quality which I did not possess, and that was that he could easily conceptualize problems in an orderly fashion. Not only did he go to all of the lectures in the University that were important for us, but he also worked them out in such a fantastic way that actually his notes could have been printed and published. When it came time to prepare for my exams, he would always lend me these notebooks, and they were my savior. What I would have done without these books I would rather not speculate on.

Despite the fact that I had this tremendous help, though, and despite the fact that everything discussed was of great importance to me, it still required quite an effort on my part to learn all of these things thoroughly. For people of my type, study in a university actually is not an ideal endeavor. When one is forced to eat so many good things, one can spoil his stomach as well as the appetite. The light of the "holy nosiness" can go out forever. I was lucky that my intellectual depression only lasted for one year after I had satisfactorily finished my studies.

BUCKY: This Marcel Grossman was also responsible for securing for you the position at the Patent Office in Zurich, wasn't he?

EINSTEIN: Yes, that is really the biggest favor that he ever did for me. On account of him, 1902 through 1909 were my most productive years due to the fact that I did not have to worry about a livelihood. Also, the work with technical patents was a real savior for me. It forced me to think along many lines and gave me many new ideas to think of in the line of physics.

Finally, a practical job for a person like myself is really a blessing. In contrast, an academic career in which a person is forced to produce scientific writings in great amounts creates a danger of intellectual superficiality. Only people with strong characters can resist this, so that a man with normal intelligence can produce what is expected of him. A man of this type relies for his existence on his job and not on any big new ideas that he may develop. Should somebody have good ideas, he can develop them as a sideline as long as he fulfills the duties of his regular job.

The main advantage of this arrangement, of course, is that if you depend upon developing new ideas for your livelihood, you always have the fear of failure, which is not the case with a regular job. In my case, I became accustomed to my work quite fast, and in a short time I was able to do a full day's work in only two or three hours. The remaining part of the day, I would work out my own ideas, which later, of course, became the Relativity Theory. Whenever anybody would come by, I would cram my notes into my desk drawer and pretend to work on my office work.

BUCKY: Did you maintain your friendship with Grossman?

EINSTEIN: I saw him occasionally. He was never very keen on physics. His field was mathematics and he very soon became professor of mathematics at the Swiss Polytechnikum. In 1912 I visited him and I will never forget how he made a very apropos remark in reference to his feelings about physics. He said, "I admit that the study of physics has helped me and I have profited from it."

As an example, he told me this story: He said, "In former times when I would sit on a chair where somebody had sat before and I still felt on the chair the warmth of his body, I felt a little uneasy about the situation. Now, in a situation of this type, this old feeling of mine no longer exists because physics has taught me that warmth or heat is something which is completely non-personal.

BUCKY: You were once quoted as saying, "With fame, I have become more stupid, which, of course, is a very common phenomenon. There is far too great a disproportion between what one is, what one isn't, and what others think one is. With me every peep becomes a trumpet solo." Where do you feel the disproportion resides between your public image and the real you?

EINSTEIN: I think that people generally overestimate me. I realize of course, the value of my contributions to science, but I don't consider myself superior or different from any other men. I really feel that I was just luckier for having been able to develop certain ideas that others before me had overlooked.

BUCKY: But surely you must account for the fact that you are so much more gifted than the average human being?

EINSTEIN: What makes you say such a foolish thing? I am not more gifted than the average human being. If you know anything about history, you would know this is so—what hard times I had in studying and the fact that I do not have a memory like some other people do. No, this is not the answer.

But if you wish, I can tell you what the answer is. I am not more gifted than anybody else. I am just more curious than the average person and I will not give up on a problem until I have found the proper solution. This is one of my greatest satisfactions in life—solving problems—and the harder they are, the more satisfaction do I get out of them. Maybe you could consider me a bit more patient in continuing with my problems than is the average human being. Now, if you understand what I have just told you, you see that it is not a matter of being more gifted but a matter of being more curious and maybe more patient until you solve a problem.

BUCKY: This all sounds very modest, coming from the greatest scientist of the twentieth century.

EINSTEIN: I just think that I cause too much bother and work to my fellow man and that is why I like to lead as simple a life as is possible. After all, most of the things that I do are done because my nature drives me to do it. So why, then, should other people give me so much respect and devotion for things that I have done when I did them solely for the purpose of my own drive?

BUCKY: Then you are not at all self-conscious about the work you do, or aware of the publicity that you generate?

EINSTEIN: One is not really aware of his own existence as much as other people who observe him. What does a fish know about the water in which he is swimming all of his life? He never really knows what happens outside of his own domain. It's the same with hatred, for instance. I am so well aware that there are certain people who hate me, but I cannot truthfully say that this touches me because I feel almost as if that feeling comes from an entirely different world with which I have no contact. This is why I have lived my life for the most part in solitude, which, I must admit, is painful during the early years, but which becomes more and more agreeable and pleasant during the years of maturity.

BUCKY: What, in the long run, then, would you say motivates you?

EINSTEIN: My scientific work is motivated by an irresistible longing to understand the secrets of nature and by no other feelings. My love for social justice and my striving to contribute toward the improvement of the human condition are quite independent of my scientific interests.

BUCKY: You were aware of the reputation that your theories have of being so esoteric as to be inaccessible to the ordinary person. What do you have to offer in this regard?

EINSTEIN: In some respects, my Theory of Relativity was elementary. As I once told a journalist, it boils down to this: When a man is in the company of a pretty girl for about an hour, it seems to him like a few seconds, but let him sit on a hot stove for only a few seconds, and it seems to him like an hour. That is, in my opinion, relativity. I do not at all believe the general consensus that my theory is so difficult that only a few people in the world are capable of understanding it.

I think that any student who is sincere about his work and who has a basic knowledge of theoretical physics should have no problem whatsoever understanding the ideas behind my

30

Relativity Theory. I think probably what happened was that a mystique began to grow around my theory. After all, the thought that a beam of light under certain conditions could actually be observed to be bending or the idea that space itself is curved were new ideas which could cause a great deal of consternation on the part of some while, on the other hand, it could contribute to bringing me great fame. But it all comes back to the mystique. Anything in the universe that is shrouded in mystery is of great interest to the average man. Therefore, when someone comes along and attempts to demystify it all, he immediately becomes the object of great curiosity, and his fame and popularity spreads.

BUCKY: What would you say has been your major goal throughout your life?

EINSTEIN: Without a doubt, I can say the quest for truth. This has not been easy, but it has been satisfying. I know from my own painful searching, with its many blind alleys, how hard it is to take a reliable step, be it ever so small, towards the understanding of what is truly significant.

BUCKY: Besides music, is there any other hobby or avocation that you enjoy when you are not involved with your serious work?

EINSTEIN: I love to reconstruct proofs of mathematical and physical theorems that I have long known. I don't do this with any goal in mind but to indulge in the pleasant occupation of thinking.

BUCKY: How would you like to be remembered?

EINSTEIN: I was once very honored by a statement that George Bernard Shaw made at a dinner that we both attended. Shaw said, "There have been many dictators who have made themselves great empires. But I am going to talk now about people who arc much more rare, namely, the ones who actually made our universe. These people, in comparison to the dictators, cannot account for any bloodstains of their fellowmen." Then he listed a handful of people in the last 3,000 years who fit this category—Galileo, Copernicus, Ptolemy, Pythagorus, Newton, Aristotle, and myself. That, I guess, is how I would like to go down in history.

BUCKY: You have often given opinions in areas which were outside of your expertise, and yet you are normally so modest and attempt to avoid publicity. Why?

EINSTEIN: Peter, I fully realize that many people listen to me not because they agree with me or because they like me particularly, but because I am Einstein. If a man has this rare capacity to have such esteem with his fellow men, then it is his obligation and duty to use this power to do good for his fellow men. For this reason, I have used every opportunity to help the underdog but, of course, only under the condition that the person is within his rights. It has given me a great joy and satisfaction to have had this power.

BUCKY: You have been so kind to consent to "going on the couch," as it were, for this discussion.

EINSTEIN: Please, you bring to mind a time when I met a psychiatrist at a party who suggested that it would be very interesting and advantageous to him if he could have the honor of psychoanalyzing me. To this suggestion, I responded, "I regret that I cannot accede to your request because I would like very much to remain in the darkness of not having been analyzed."

CHAPTER TWO

Einstein in America

1. The Princeton Years

Resettling from the Old World to the New has usually been a shocking experience for most cultivated Europeans. The brash, robust, noisy, energetic panorama that prevailed always presented a clash with the more proper, staid, traditionalist, and slow-moving Continental style. Everything must appear totally alien to such a sensibility. This was as true in the pre-World War II days as it still is today.

If the immigrant chose a cosmopolitan center, he would step into a world of Art Deco skyscrapers and an ethnic melting pot considerably removed from his native memories of medieval, homogenous cities. If, instead, he veered toward the outskirts, the scene that he was likely to encounter would be pleasing to the eye, perhaps, but culturally somewhat of a wasteland. (Or, as Gertrude Stein somewhat bitingly put it: "In the United States today, there is more space where nobody is than where anybody is. That is what makes America what it is." Stein's rival for piercing wit, Dorothy Parker, had characterized even a big city like Oakland, California, this way: "The trouble with Oakland is, there's no *there* there.")

So, where to go? Could any European emigrating to the United States hope to recreate the conditions of his homeland? (In the 1970's, Aleksandr Solzhenitsyn, exiled from the Soviet Union, solved the problem by sealing himself in a tract of several hundred acres in beautiful Vermont, which recreated for him the vastness of his native Russia.) Luckily, for Albert Einstein, fate had a hand in selecting for him perhaps the most congenial spot for a man of his gentle nature. And that spot—most unlikely of all—turned out to be in New Jersey.

There are two conceptions of New Jersey—one a domestic, the

other an outsider's image. To most Americans, New Jersey—or "New Joi-sey," as many will say, mocking the accent of some Jersey Citians—is epitomized by the "Turnpike belt," that narrow corridor of steaming, choking chimneys, oil refineries, and industrial dumping grounds that winds out of New York City southwest to Trenton—a fifty-mile stretch that seems to put the lie to New Jersey's official designation as "the Garden State."

To most foreigners, on the other hand—those who have heard of it at all—New Jersey conjures up images of one gigantic suburb, a way-station between New York and Philadelphia.

Both of these images are true in their own way, but they are very incomplete. For in focusing on the evident, they overlook the many subtleties of this small but populous state.

They overlook the picturesque hills around the Gladstone-Peapack area that attract the horsey set for English-style riding and horse breeding. They overlook quaint old towns like Morristown, Mt. Bethel and Chatham that are brimming with history and facing a restless, hectic, modern world with quiet dignity. They overlook the sinewy seacoast, stretching southward some one hundred miles, hosting ocean towns as diverse as Seaside Park, gaudy mecca of the penny arcade fiends; Spring Lake, dignified haven for those who take their ocean with a pinch of peace, or Harvey Cedars, sanctuary of the nouveau riche—all, by the way, within twenty miles of each other. And they overlook the genteel college towns that dot the state—places like Convent Station, Glassboro, New Brunswick, Madison, and Princeton.

Princeton—of all New Jersey towns, this is the one that would appeal most to those who appreciate a European aura. From its serene business streets (all two of them) to the regal English-style architecture of the university's older campus buildings to the hilly roads winding through enclaves of privilege, to the cultural amenities and French restaurants so alien to most other New Jersey suburban communities, Princeton carries a European flavor found in few other American cities, as if Oxford had been lifted and transported whole across the ocean.

Walking along the easy streets of Princeton, one feels the ghosts and legends of age following one's tracks. There behind you walks Woodrow Wilson, once President, not only of the United States but also of Princeton University. Across the street, Svetlana Alliluyeva, Stalin's daughter, window shops. Walking a bit farther up the road, conversing with a friend, is the famous anthropologist, Ashley Montagu. And, yes, there ahead of you, wrapped in an old tattered coat, hair waving in the breeze, deep in thought, head bowed, walks the ghost of Albert Einstein.

That figure wasn't always a ghost, of course. For almost twenty-two years, Einstein, the man, was a living presence in this university town. He came to Princeton in the autumn of 1933, trading the intellectual desolation and physical dangers of Nazi Germany for a life of security in a country alien in spirit to many Europeans.

One of the first people that the Einsteins contacted within days of their arrival in Princeton was my mother, who had sent a telegram of welcome immediately upon their landing. The following two letters, written by Elsa Einstein to my mother, offer some insight into the Einsteins' state of mind upon making the big step of emigrating to America:

10/17/33

Dear Mrs. Bucky,

I want to thank you very much for your telegram of greetings. We arrived in Princeton today. When we landed, we used all kinds of tricks to evade the newspaper reporters. On the dock, there were many people who wanted to see my husband. It was preferred that he arrive very quietly in these troubled times, so we had to avoid all crowds. This is absolutely essential for his security.

We live in a hotel (The Peacock Inn) until November 1, and then we go into a furnished home that we have rented. I will be happy to see you again. Please let me know when you can come.

With my heartiest regards,
Elsa

10/21/33

Dear Mrs. Bucky,

Nobody can escape his fate. In Berlin, you always took care of us, which I will never forget. We used your care and we took too much of your valuable time, which people always do when people are as good-hearted as you are.

And now since we have arrived in the United States, the same thing is happening again. Due to your extreme kindness, we are causing you too much trouble. Is it not peculiar that things go that way? Along these lines, I would be very happy if Mister Peter would pick me up and I would like to do it at the earliest opportunity, either on Monday or Tuesday. It would be a great favor to me if Mister Peter could meet me there. I would then take the railroad to New York and would let Peter know on which train I will arrive. And then, if he would be kind enough to pick me up at the railroad station where I will give him further particulars and he can take me to the dentist. And then, after the dentist, I will come quickly to you for about a half-hour before going back to Princeton. I wouldn't want to see anyone else in New York at this time. I have too many people that I know and so many invitations from people in New York, I can't even start to tell you. But you I would like to see and from the bottom of my heart, I will be happy to see you. At later times, my husband will come along with me to visit you, which we would love to do if you would permit us. My most hearty thanks for helping me with this.

We have rented a small house which is beautiful and in a nice neighborhood, and the landscaping is very nice. I don't need any help, as I took along the young girl who for many years came to my husband twice a week to be my secretary.

The house is furnished and I can take it over with everything in it. Silver, linens, and similar things I could not bring from Germany. I was not even permitted to go near my belongings. I must now learn to live with simple things such as in this house. But, you see, this is not important anymore. Where the home is situated it is so isolated and so beautiful

that I'm sure we'll be very happy in it. Margot-chen will be
here around Christmas and will stay with us for a few months.
If everything goes well, we will be here until the end of
March. Then we will go to Spain and France, where my
husband has accepted professorships.

Many hearty greetings,
Elsa

What was it like for Albert Einstein, putting down roots in a
strange land at the age of fifty-four? First of all, it wasn't a poor
life—though no thanks to Einstein's business acumen. Einstein
had been offered a position at the Institute for Advanced Studies
by Dr. Abraham Flexner, the director, who gave Einstein virtually
a blank check to write his own salary. Einstein carefully figured
out how much money he would require to live in his new country.
Translating his knowledge of German currency into American
dollars, Einstein computed that he would require $3,000 a year,
and it was this figure that he suggested to Dr. Flexner.

Fortunately for Einstein, the Institute did not accept his suggestion. Einstein, perplexed by their refusal, and assuming that he
had asked for too much, quickly asked Dr. Flexner, "Could I live
on less?" Flexner, astutely sizing up the situation, suggested that
the matter be arranged with Mrs. Einstein, who was more adept at
business affairs. At the time, Einstein's adviser and accountant,
Samuel D. Leidesdorf, spent at least an hour explaining to Einstein
the difference in buying power and the greater expenses of living
in the United States compared with Germany. But Einstein, despite
the fact that he nodded and agreed, was not entirely convinced.

Finally, the Institute offered $17,000, or almost six times his
original request. Einstein couldn't understand how he could possibly spend such an amount of money during a year's time. After
many more discussions, the Institute finally agreed to set his
salary at about $16,000—a handsome sum a half-century ago,
when the average per capita income in the area was about $1,500.

Although he is not mentioned in the major biographies of Einstein, Samuel Leidesdorf was an important figure in his life, especially so in light of the financial naiveté of the scientist.

Leidesdorf was one of the top accountants in Manhattan during

Einstein's years in America. He owned many buildings on Forty-Second Street and was responsible for raising all of the funds for New York University's Medical Center (even today, if you walk down to First Avenue and Thirty-Third Street to Leidesdorf Park, you can read a plaque highlighting his contributions).

Upon Einstein's arrival in the United States, my father contacted Leidesdorf, a personal friend, to solicit his advice and expertise on Einstein's finances. As a result, as far back as 1933, Einstein entrusted Leidesdorf with the then princely sum of $25,000 for investment. A measure of Leidesdorf's astuteness was that upon Einstein's death, his step-daughter Margot received $250,000 from that investment. Under Leidesdorf's watchful eye, in just twenty-two years Einstein's original investment had multiplied tenfold.

Of course, as a wealthy accountant, Leidesdorf was stereotypically conservative, clashing with Einstein's more liberal political stance in ways that led to some light-hearted exchanges in the correspondence between the two. For example, a year before Einstein's death and after some now-forgotten controversial public statement such as Einstein was wont to make, he had taken some ribbing from Leidesdorf. In response, Einstein wrote to Leidesdorf:

> Trembling, I reach for my pen, in the knowledge that I have, in my youthful irresponsibility, again caused
> TROUBLE
> as our good [J. Robert] Oppenheimer and my friend [Otto] Nathan clearly but kindly informed me. I console myself with the hope that my new sins will soon be forgiven by our Holy Ones and made pure by the kosher stamp. So far it hasn't happened.
>
> Your wonderful gift of flowers has assured me that your friendly feelings toward me have not been chilled by the misunderstanding.

Even up to a couple of weeks before Einstein's death, the physicist and his accountant gibed charmingly in letters they exchanged. Upon receipt of a plant sent from Leidesdorf as a birthday present, Einstein wrote the following note of thanks on March 26, 1955:

Dear Mr. Leidesdorf:

You have sent me for my birthday a highly aristocratic and sensitive plant the keeping of which means not a little responsibility. It is also a serious competition for the water-plant you gave me for my 70th birthday and which at this moment is before my eyes. I would hardly be able to keep this enterprise alive without the permanent care of my daughter who is doing it 'scientifically.'

I thank you for this new proof of your kindness to me in spite of all the 'subversive' escapades I performed over the years. . . .

Leidesdorf promised to bring a "less aristocratic" plant on his next visit, and on April 1, 1955, confirmed in a letter to Einstein that he was, instead,

having delivered to you a cactus plant, which is less aristocratic and sensitive than the one I sent you on your birthday.

I hasten to do this because I do not think you should waste your time watering plants, when you could spend it so much more profitably on "subversive" activities.

Getting back to the Institute for Advanced Studies, Einstein's obligations to the Institute were really only to himself. He was committed to be there only between October and April, and he wasn't required to teach. His main function was to research and develop his theories and ideas. Actually, the one drawback to this arrangement was that Einstein missed the collision of young intellects in the classroom environment. His work at the Institute, which has no students, threatened to isolate him from the younger college set. For this reason, he established a standing rule that allowed students from Princeton University to come to him at any time with their problems.

This underscored one of Einstein's most amazing qualities, that is, the ability to concentrate at a moment's notice on the most abstract of thoughts, to be interrupted in his work, and then to continue with his own problem without losing one strand of his thoughts.

Einstein did not attain true permanency in his new land for the first two years of his residency. He was first given quarters on the Princeton campus until he and his wife were moved to a rented house at 2 Library Place, a few hundred yards from the campus. From there, Einstein easily walked to the headquarters of the Institute, on Alexander Street, which juts out from Nassau Street, the main Princeton roadway. Finally, in August of 1935, the Einsteins bought the house at 112 Mercer Street, a simple, clapboard white colonial house on a pleasant street with quiet country-like surroundings, where Einstein was to live out the last twenty years of his life.

Anyone driving along Mercer Street today would find it difficult to imagine that here lived one of the greatest scientists of the twentieth century. The house at 112 Mercer, where Einstein's stepdaughter Margot continued to live until her own death in 1986, is modest, and old-fashioned, in keeping with Einstein's disdain for luxury. But it is easy to see that this unprepossessing house gave Einstein what he so craved—a privacy that enabled him to carry on with his work.

Einstein was determined that his house should not be preserved as a museum after his death. Indeed, it hasn't been and, in fact, Helen Dukas also continued to live there until her own death in 1982, and very little has changed to this day.

So what was it really like to be there in those exciting days when Einstein filled the house with his ideas, his mirth, and his music? Come along, then, on a guided ramble through the great scientist's house and property.

To approach the house, you must walk through a large lawned area and climb the five steps to the veranda. You do well to check the number, 112, for despite any preconceptions, Einstein's house is not very different from the others on the same street.

Stepping into the front entrance, you turn to the left to find a modest, 15-foot-square living room, in which the ghostly echoes of many vital discussions between Einstein and his friends can almost be heard. Two windows grace this room, which affords views of Mercer Street and a neighboring house. The furniture in the room, as, indeed, in all the rooms throughout the house, is heavy, antique, and very Germanic. This is the very furniture that

Einstein had had shipped from his Haberlandstrasse home in Berlin, and it contrasted sharply with the styles that prevailed in most of the other homes in this Princeton neighborhood. Actually, it is thought that Einstein despised this furniture but that his wife, Elsa, was enamored of it and asked the Nazi government to release it for shipment when they emigrated from Germany.

Adjoining the living room toward the rear of the house is the dining room, the largest room of the house, about fifteen-by-twenty-five feet. Here sits a long, antique dining table, and on one wall is a functional, old-fashioned fireplace. It is in this room that you get a sense of the house's age, as the ceiling gradually lowers near the back of the house and the old, wide-board floors sag. At first glance, you expect this room to be well lit, as there are four windows. Still, a darkness seems to hang there like a stubborn fog because of extensive greenery outside that filters out the sunlight.

Passing an old cabinet containing many dishes, you push through a small, swinging door into a fairly modern kitchen, about twelve by fifteen feet. Two windows provide the kitchen with light—one looking out to the long, narrow back garden, and the other out toward a neighboring house.

One small lavatory off the kitchen contains a small sink. One wonders how a man of Einstein's substantial frame could have negotiated this lavatory. To close the door, you must push yourself toward the far wall. After going through the same contortions to exit from this tiny room, you walk out into the main foyer that extends from the lavatory all the way to the front door. Retracing your steps to the front entrance, you turn to the other side of the house.

Here you enter another small living room, which was the workroom of Helen Dukas. This is more like what you would expect to find in the great physicist's home: bookshelves line the room from floor to ceiling. In this room sits the only telephone that Einstein had. Had you dialed "Princeton 1606" when he was living there, you might have been greeted with a friendly hello from one of the most eminent men of the century.

Beyond this workroom, you enter Einstein's sanctuary—his music room, containing a grand piano. A small picture window helped make this room a pleasant setting for Einstein's many evenings of string quartets and other chamber music.

41

Returning to the front of the house again, you begin to climb a wide staircase to the second floor and a working room built by Einstein shortly after he moved in. Half of its back wall was replaced by a huge picture window that seemed to bring the rear garden into his study. Einstein once said of this room, "I do not actually feel as being within a building."

This is the room to which he retreated to ponder his theories. On two sides were walls covered with bookcases from floor to ceiling. In the middle was a large table, covered with pencils, papers and a number of pipes. His working time was divided between this table, his desk, which looked out over the garden, and his favorite easy chair. It was when he really got down to his serious work that Einstein preferred to sit in this chair, often with work papers propped on a knee. The only decorations in the study were portraits of the physicists James Maxwell and Michael Faraday and Mohandas K. Gandhi and a certificate citing Einstein as an honorary member of the city of Bern's Nature Research Organization. Certainly, it was a very functional room, in keeping with Einstein's avoidance of unnecessary luxury.

On either side of the study are two bedrooms, one of them Einstein's, the other that of Helen Dukas. Toward the center of the second floor, you pass a bathroom with modern furnishings through which you can enter either Einstein's bedroom or, through a second door, his step-daughter Margot's small studio, a room of about ten by fifteen feet. This studio opened into Margot's bedroom, the window of which faced onto Mercer Street. Finally, one other bedroom, facing Mercer Street, belonged to Einstein's sister, Maja.

Back down the staircase, you come again to the foyer, through which you walk back toward the kitchen. The rear door leads you onto a pleasant veranda, roofed in for protection from the elements. Stepping off the veranda, you walk out onto a pleasant, tree-shaded garden with a distinctly country flavor enhanced by tall hedges that obscure visibility of anything but the garden itself.

Numerous trees—elms, maples, and weeping willows—dot the lawn, while on one side a small grape arbor vies with lilies for attention. To the back of the garden a small flower garden provides scenic distraction, sharing its bed of earth with a tiny vegetable patch of which Einstein was exceedingly proud.

One can well imagine the serenity that this simple home and garden provided for Einstein. Indeed, most of his days were spent here on Mercer Street. Since Einstein's duties at the Institute did not involve teaching, his schedule was his own to make. Usually, he would work at the Institute's headquarters only in the morning. Then, around noontime, he and his associates would walk back together to Mercer Street in a neighborhood where most of his colleagues also lived. Dr. Alan Schenstone, chairman of the Princeton Physics Department, lived directly opposite Einstein on Mercer.

Schenstone once described a typical noon-time scene on the street, with Einstein and several colleagues walking up Mercer, engaged in intense conversation. In front of Einstein's house they continued to talk, hands and arms in motion. Suddenly, the discussion ended, the group broke up to go their separate ways and Einstein, still deep in a trance of concentration, forgetting his surroundings, turned around and began to walk back to the Institute until Miss Dukas, observing from a window, ran out and dragged the professor back to his house for lunch.

Lunch for Einstein in Princeton, as in Germany, was his main meal of the day, at which he usually enjoyed Italian food, a holdover from boyhood days when he lived in Milan with his parents. Spaghetti or macaroni often sufficed to satisfy him.

After lunch, Einstein would go to his study either to take a nap or to resume work. In the evening, he would take a light supper, consisting of sandwiches with no warm foods. Then, he would either entertain guests for conversation or music or return to his study, sometimes not to emerge until far into the night.

Einstein, of course, was famous in his community, although there was not the constant frenzy of celebrity that we have come to expect now. And this was how Einstein liked it. He loved the quiet town and went to it because he felt that he could live and, most important, do his work there free from the rush of the big city. It suited him fine that he could walk to and from the Institute without attracting crowds of curiosity-seekers and autograph-hunters.

In the early days, it is true, he encountered a certain coldness. Princeton, an Ivy League school, was an enclave of WASP-dom and Einstein was a Jew—and an eccentric Jew, at that, with his long hair and his lack of concern about matters of dress. But time convinced Princetonians that Einstein only enhanced their community.

So, the man who for many years had floated between Italy, Germany, and Switzerland, settled finally in this tiny, eastern corner of the United States, for the first time putting down true roots. There he worked and played and observed his new homeland, trying to make sense of a society that had attracted so many millions of Europeans like himself for so many years. His observations were always frank, but one could always be sure that they stemmed from his eternal quest for truth and logic.

2. Conversation: Thoughts on America

BUCKY: Professor, you spent more than the first fifty years of your life living in Europe. To suddenly emigrate to the United States must have been a traumatic experience. What were your first impressions?

EINSTEIN: Actually, I always felt very happy living in America, because I think that it is a wonderful country to live in. I have always considered myself fortunate to be here and also to have been given the privilege of becoming an American citizen.

Probably my greatest impression when I first arrived was one of gratification to see that so much money was made available for scientific research here. To me this demonstrated that the United States was not just content to develop the country as a whole but had an honest and true desire to explore the natural sciences. In fact, the longer I live here the more I truly believe that this is one of the greatest assets that we possess—the will to learn and to understand the natural wonders of this world.

BUCKY: You say: "One of the greatest assets." What do you count as some of the other assets of America—the country or its people?

EINSTEIN: Oh, of course, there are many others. As individuals, for example, everyone feels assured of his worth as an individual, no matter what level of wealth or poverty. Nobody in America bows down to another person or class. Certainly, there are great discrepancies of wealth, as in other countries, and this wealth means superior power to those who possess it.

But somehow, in America, this isn't allowed to undermine the healthy self-confidence and natural respect for the dignity of each individual. And yet, this strong individualistic current is well-balanced by the need for community. In fact, it is my impression that in the United States, "we" is much more stressed than "I," which is exactly the opposite than in Europe. This is a basic American strength, I think. Generally speaking, Americans are kinder to each other than the average European and there is more unity in their philosophies.

BUCKY: Surely, though, you must have some criticisms to make of America and Americans?

EINSTEIN: Well, of course, I see things that I do not care for, but everything cannot be perfect. I actually find it difficult to criticize anything in America publicly because I am, after all, a guest of this country and for this reason would not like to have my criticisms misunderstood. But yes, naturally, there are imperfections that I see. For example, I think the United States is considerably more materialistic than European countries.

This materialism fosters a certain mentality that I have carefully avoided. There is, for instance, a certain amount of superficiality that is predominant in the United States. This external quest for material comfort and economic security contributes to this superficiality of thought and feelings. It takes a strong will for a foreigner to avoid being sucked into this maelstrom. Another weakness of this country is the tendency to try to legislate moral principles. For example, I think that Prohibition was definitely a bad thing for this country.

BUCKY: You don't think that it might have been a good thing for people's health or for families in general?

EINSTEIN: This is not really the point, whether it was good law or

45

bad law. The point is, as a general principle, any law that cannot be enforced is a worthless law. Also, the Prohibition laws directly resulted in an increase in crime and the growth of organized crime. I also feel that those laws had a stultifying effect on public discourse because people didn't gather as much in public places. I don't think that different ideas and views on public affairs by individuals can be exchanged quite as freely and efficiently as in a public place.

BUCKY: So, all in all, you feel that there is more to be pleased with in America than to be displeased with?

EINSTEIN: Ah, yes, my friend. Look, the European in general is much more of a pessimist than the American. The average European is not particularly helpful and certainly is much less kindhearted than the American. The average American has a greater social attitude than the average European. By this I mean that he is much more helpful and kinder to his fellow man.

BUCKY: Isn't that a contradiction, in a sense? What I mean to suggest is, if Americans have such a strong individualist streak, how can they maintain at the same time a cooperative social attitude?

EINSTEIN: It seems like a contradiction, but it isn't, in fact. Americans are individualistic in the sense that they recognize the individual dignity and worth of each human being, regardless of his social position. But Americans—and Asiatics, too, I should add—are not individualistic from the eccentric standpoint. You find many more eccentrics—thus, true individuals—among the Europeans. But it is this recognition of individual dignity that creates among the American populace a desire to ensure that everyone is treated fairly.

BUCKY: And yet, we have the uncomfortable situation of the Negroes and how they have been treated in this country.

EINSTEIN: Yes, that is true. This is one of the unfortunate contradictions of America. The longer I live in America, the more sad I feel about this situation. I have spoken with many people who have told me that they had bad feelings against Negroes because of unfavorable experiences that they had by living side by side with them. I've also been told that Negroes are not equal in intelligence or in their sense of reliability and that they are irresponsible.

But I think that there is a certain amount of selfishness in this belief. By that I mean that American ancestors took these black people forcibly from their homes so that the white man could more easily acquire wealth. By suppressing and exploiting and degrading black people into slavery, the white man was able to have an easier life. I really think that it is from a result of a desire to maintain this condition that modern prejudices stem.

BUCKY: Is there any relation between this anti-Negro sentiment and anti-Semitism?

EINSTEIN: Only that it is part of the continuing story of man's inhumanity. Look, as far back as Greek times, people kept slaves. The only difference then was that the slaves were white people and therefore could not be degraded due to racial differences. And yet, the Greek philosophers declared these slaves to be inferior. They, too, were deprived of their liberty. However, being a Jew myself, perhaps I can understand and empathize with how black people feel as victims of discrimination.

BUCKY: What do you think can be done in the long run to solve the problem?

EINSTEIN: Well, there is no magic solution. I would only hope that where there is a will there is a way. I think probably that Americans will have to realize how stupid this attitude is and how harmful it is, also, to the standing of the United States. After all, every country is supposed to be looking up to this country. But I think that if individuals are really honest with themselves about this problem, they would undoubtedly recognize how wrong this bias really is.

BUCKY: You mentioned earlier that much money was available for scientific research in America. What about the quality of science here?

EINSTEIN: Oh, I think there is a tremendous superiority within the technical fields in the United States. I think that the funds available might be one explanation, but also I think that the art of organizing seems to have been developed to the highest degree in the United States.

BUCKY: Do you think that this superiority prevails in fields other than science?

EINSTEIN: Yes, of course, you see, the American is, on the whole, much more practical than the European in most aspects of everyday life. For example, most houses in America are much more practically designed than in Europe.

BUCKY: You don't see this as more of an economic imperative than practicality?

EINSTEIN: You are right in the sense that because the cost of labor is so much higher here, Americans must take short cuts in building. But still, the practical element must be there in order to conquer this problem. Anyway, I feel that this tendency is a correct one. I welcome the idea that labor for everyday needs and wants can be reduced so that the individual can have more time to devote to himself.

Yes, you're quite right in saying that the high cost of labor has resulted in technical improvements. Compare this to some of the Asiatic countries, which are way over-populated in comparison to the United States. Because the cost of labor is comparatively low there, machinery has not been developed to any high degree. Europe, on the other hand, is just about in between the United States and Asia.

BUCKY: The Germans, too, though, are highly skilled in scientific and technical areas and have, also, almost a mystical devotion to the cult of the leader. I myself fear that this poses a threat to the United States, particularly as there is such an isolationist strain here.

EINSTEIN: Ah, dear Mr. Peter, you forget one important thing, though, that this country possesses, which is of extreme importance in winning a war and which I have always admired.

BUCKY: And what is that, Professor?

EINSTEIN: The ability in this country to convert their peacetime industry into a wartime economy within the shortest period of time. I guess, as you were only a toddler, you don't remember the last war (World War I). You are correct to be concerned about isolationism here. It is very dangerous. Americans must realize that in the modern world, there are no more barriers.

The ocean is no longer protection in a world of airplanes. Americans will have to come to terms with this and realize that as one of the largest and most powerful countries in the world, it has a much greater responsibility for international affairs than any other country.

BUCKY: So you do not fear for America against the threat of Hitler?

EINSTEIN: Of course there is fear in such matters. But what I mean to say is that America, with its great practical abilities and organizational skills can generate a powerful military power of its own. Also, Americans have a tremendous optimism that enables them to overcome great odds. This is a quality that makes me feel very much at home.

I often think that Americans are like big children, children who are always happy. They have the typical optimistic outlook of all children, they're kind and friendly. Perhaps, if they are lacking one thing, it is self-confidence. But most importantly, they have this natural optimistic outlook and no envy of others. One only has to look at newspaper pictures in the United States to discover that nearly every face is smiling in comparison to the dour European newspaper photographs.

BUCKY: Well, of course, most people are asked to smile when these photographs are taken.

EINSTEIN: Well, I can't just imagine anybody smiling for a newspaper photograph just because he is asked to if he is in a bad mood.

BUCKY: What do you think is the reason for the apparent economic superiority of the United States?

EINSTEIN: Again, I think that the organization and management of labor is set up much more practically in the United States and certainly with much less trouble and friction than is the case in Europe. This is even true in universities and in private organizations, such as charities. Private enterprise seems also to be directly responsible for some of our most important cultural developments, in comparison to Europe, where these things are more influenced by government. For instance, telephones, railways and radio, and even many schools are predominantly in private hands in America. I also think that a strong contributing factor to this is public opinion, which is so highly valued in this country. On account of this, wealthy people are more or less obliged, if they want to be successful in their communities, to spend not only a considerable amount of their wealth for the public good, but even to give some of their own time to public problems, especially those problems arising in the communities in which they live.

CHAPTER THREE

The German Experiment

1. Making the Best of It in Germany

Einstein was a citizen of the world, it is true. To great men, particularly in the arts and sciences, it is common that nationalism is not as important as establishing a common humanity. Einstein, as one of these, truly lived for his science.

But he was, if only for the historical record, a German, and although he had forsaken his native land for Switzerland early in life, the call of his science brought him back to Berlin, where he spent the years from 1927 to 1933.

The irony of Einstein's situation is that that which caused him to leave Germany the first time, in 1901—i.e., Germany's militarism and ethnic intolerance—was the very thing that sent him fleeing again, this time in 1933, to the United States.

But it is instructive in getting to know Einstein to pause to reflect upon his life in pre-Hitler Germany—his likes and dislikes, his daily routine, his social life, his work, and his play.

Einstein's home in Berlin was an elaborate seven-room apartment on the Haberlandstrasse. It was quite a luxurious place for the time, with an elevator and a porter who carefully screened visitors. This was the closest thing to an American doorman, which at the time was an unknown entity in European cities.

Einstein's apartment was on the fourth floor, but it also had a small room on the fifth floor that was called the Tower Room. There, Einstein worked in seclusion, his only compromise with privacy being a telephone. One wall of this room was filled from floor to ceiling with books, and two tiny windows provided all of the light.

Next to Einstein's desk was a large telescope with which Einstein observed the night skies around Berlin. On his wall were three pictures—those of the physicists Faraday and Maxwell and the philosopher Arthur Schopenhauer. On several occasions, Einstein sat for his own portrait in the Tower Room.

The apartment also had a library in which Einstein kept all of his books except references, which he kept close at hand in the Tower Room. All of the bookshelves were open, except for one rack that was enclosed with glass doors. In keeping with Einstein's simple nature, his library was sparsely furnished, with only a small table, a few straight chairs and one comfortable lounge chair. In front of the window was a desk on top of which sat a large globe. Jutting out from the library was a large balcony, which Einstein seldom used.

Bordering this library was Einstein's bedroom, which was also simply appointed, with only his bed, one small night table and a few chairs. One oddity in this bedroom was a small table with large drawers that stood next to the door and contained twenty-four settings of silverware.

Despite the fact that the Victrola had long been invented and that Einstein was a great lover of music, he had a distaste for "canned music" at this time and refused to have a record player in his home. He had an acute sense of hearing and the primitive state of this invention carried with it too many extraneous noises. Only later, when recordings were refined and much clearer, did he accept a record player that colleagues at Princeton University gave him.

He had one radio, which Einstein also disliked. But Margot and the Einsteins' maid, Herta (who was called Herta-chen by Elsa's daughters) used to enjoy sitting in front of the radio and listening to quiz shows, a popular genre of the day (at which Herta was superior to Margot).

Einstein had many friends in Berlin but none of his friends would visit him without first telephoning for an appointment. He had many telephone extensions in this apartment, but most of the telephone calls were handled by Mrs. Einstein except for very private matters or anything to do with Einstein's work or science. Those would be handled by Einstein himself, in his Tower Room. For posterity's sake, the famous telephone number was: "COrnelius 2807."

Many notable visitors made their way to Einstein's apartment during these years, including Charlie Chaplin, who after visiting in 1931, described the place as a very small apartment with worn-out carpets. Einstein, though, could be very firm about socializing against his will. Once, when his wife invited someone against his wishes while Einstein was meeting with the Russian physicist H.F. Joffe, he set off with Joffe for a nearby park and worked with him there for four hours, until the intruder had departed. The two scientists then resumed their work in the Tower Room.

Einstein's visitors at this time were a veritable social register of some of the most important scientists and cultural figures of the day. Among them were many Nobel Prize winners, including the chemists Walter Nernst and Fritz Haber, the physicist Max Planck, the poet and playwright Gerhart Hauptmann, and the Indian poet Rabindranath Tagore (who would visit Einstein only in his summer home in Caputh). The eccentric, cigar-smoking actress Hedwig Wengel also visited, as did the musical director Erich Kleiber.

As in America in his later years, Einstein had to contend in Germany with publicity-seekers, cranks, and hangers-on. His wife, Elsa, did everything she could to shield him from such types, but she occasionally failed.

The British Ambassador to Berlin, Sir Horace Rumbold, once told me an amusing anecdote about his young son who had come to Berlin on a visit to his father. Immediately upon his arrival, the boy asked Rumbold, "Daddy, have you met Einstein yet?" When Sir Horace told him that, indeed, he had not, his son shot him a look of great consternation as if to imply that his father had not as yet fulfilled his most important diplomatic function.

On one occasion, Mrs. Einstein told Albert that there were two orthodox Jews who she assumed were begging for money, waiting outside to see him. Einstein, always a supporter of the underdog, was moved to let the two men in. Once inside, speaking a mixture of Yiddish and Hebrew, they told him that they were businessmen who had walked all the way from Warsaw, Poland, to see him. When Einstein asked why they had walked so far, they answered strangely that they did not like to ride in the bowels of the earth, as they called the underground lines. It got even stranger, though, as they then told Einstein that their mission was to see the "King of the Soul." It had been revealed to them, they said, that if they accomplished this their lives would be prolonged. Once they had explained this, the two men left, apparently satisfied that they had fulfilled their mission. "The King of the Soul" was extremely amused.

On another occasion, the Berlin police called Elsa and told her that they had arrested a derelict who insisted that every night at a certain time in a certain pub, he would meet Einstein. Elsa tried to assure the police that Einstein hardly ever left the house at night, usually opting to read a book or play the violin. Nevertheless, the police insisted that he and his wife file a written declaration before they would close the case.

Einstein's staff in Berlin consisted of two people—a maid and a secretary, a position that rotated between several law students (because of their notorious habit of cutting classes they were the only students with time enough to take on this duty) until Helen Dukas came on the scene—to remain with him until his death.

Einstein's maid, Herta, stayed with him through all of the Berlin years. Einstein called her "Die Stramme Herta"—the strong Herta—a testament to her willingness to take on the heaviest work. She helped serve large parties and cleaned the apartment besides bringing him his tea every day.

But Herta became more than a maid to Einstein. She screened many of his incoming telephone calls, and occasionally, when Einstein would relent and sit for a portrait, he would even use Herta as an expert on whether the painting was doing justice to him. Besides, she knew where his misplaced books could be found. (Once, after she had pulled out a book from the Tower Room that he had been looking for in vain, Einstein said that Herta knew his books better than his own secretary. But, of course, this was no accident, for Herta dusted all of the books every week, and she was allowed to take any book she wanted out of Einstein's library, a privilege that she made use of often.)

Once, after a trip to Berlin, she missed her bus connection to Caputh, Einstein's summer home. It was late at night, and during a two-hour walk from the railroad station she was justifiably scared. As if to fulfill her premonitions, a dog jumped out at her and frightened her. When she finally reached Caputh, she maintained that the waves in her hair had been straightened by the incident. When Einstein heard this, he laughed, saying, "I have heard that if somebody gets frightened, they get white hair, but I never knew that you can lose the waves in your hair through fright!"

Einstein was kind to Herta and treated her like family. Once, for instance, when she noticed that he subscribed to a magazine called *The New Russia,* she mentioned that her older brother would be interested in reading back issues if Einstein would save them. He immediately gave her brother a subscription. Einstein also once gave him busts of Goethe and Schiller, which Herta's brother prized.

Another time, when Herta was hospitalized, the Einsteins sent her home to recuperate with her family and paid her full wages for the period. Then, when she returned to work, they hired additional help to lighten her chores.

Herta had her own room in the Berlin apartment, with a bed, a washstand, and a closet. But if Einstein and Margot were away on a trip, Herta would be asked to sleep in the guest room, to be near Elsa in case she required assistance.

Although Herta's official title was "helper to the lady of the house," she really ran the house and cooked as well. But it was indicative of Einstein's concern for her that, when the family held parties, they usually hired someone extra to come in and wash dishes. They would also hire others to wash windows.

Herta's salary started at 45 marks a week but soon rose to 60 marks (the price of a good dress at that time was about 20 marks). In addition, her living expenses were provided, and she received tips from guests whom she escorted down the elevator to unlock the night door. Generally for this she was tipped one mark, although one generous guest, a Mr. Goldman, often tipped her ten marks. Also, Mrs. Einstein would allow Herta, who loved coffee, to buy a quarter-pound a week for herself, while the professor was only allowed to drink decaffeinated coffee.

Herta had a free afternoon every week and a Sunday off every two weeks (besides a lot of other free Sundays when the Einsteins were away). In addition to her salary, Herta would be given two marks extra for any day that the Einsteins were away so that she could either buy food to cook or go to a restaurant. At Christmas, even though they were Jewish, they would also give Herta—a Christian—her own tree and either fifty marks or sewing material for clothing.

The Einsteins also allowed Herta to invite guests, such as her brother, to the apartment. On these occasions, they would give the dining room over to her and her guests and then retreat into other rooms.

Despite their kindnesses, there were often clashes of will between the maid and Mrs. Einstein, arguments that usually demanded all of the diplomacy that Elsa's two daughters could muster. Ilse would usually bring presents to Herta so that she wouldn't quit. It was indicative of his tendency to help the underdog that, whenever Herta and his wife argued, Einstein would take Herta's side.

For a time, Einstein made occasional summer journeys to the sea for recreation and he would often stay at the estate of Professor Janos Plesch in Gatow, a suburb of Berlin. (Professor Plesch, who at the time was one of Einstein's personal physicians and who later became the private physician of Sir Winston Churchill, once told Herta that she should keep detailed notes of her employment with the Einsteins so that she could later convert them into a book. Alas, Herta did not take Plesch's advice.)

The one drawback of Plesch's estate was that it was surrounded by large, swampy fields that brought an offensive odor whenever the wind blew in the wrong direction. One day, the Mayor of Berlin came to visit Plesch and to talk with Einstein. During their meal, the Mayor asked Einstein whether the foul odor bothered him. Einstein replied with characteristic wit: "No, it doesn't bother me at all, because sometimes I get even."

To commemorate Einstein's fiftieth birthday, in 1929, the city of Berlin decided to give him land in Caputh, near the soon-to-be-famous town of Potsdam, for a summer home. Einstein became irritated before this transaction was completed as bureaucratic details and red tape added delay upon delay. In the end, Einstein, himself, bought a lot adjoining the proposed gift site so that the house would connect with the main part of the Waldstrasse.

The resulting summer house, constructed of unpainted wood, had a bright red roof and white-lacquered window frames. Besides an open terrace, the house had six rooms including a workroom next to his bedroom and a glassed-in dining room. The living room opened onto a large porch filled with comfortable chairs, and the terrace had large glass doors, which were always left open. This led, via three or four steps, down to the garden, which was terraced in several layers, and through the middle of all of this ran a walking path.

The Einsteins did not garden in Caputh but hired a gardener instead. According to one account, Einstein gave the job to a man named Meyer, a typesetter who was out of work because of his politics—he was a social democrat. Einstein, hearing of his problem, hired him so that he could support his family. (This was typical of Einstein's consideration for those in need. For example, although he hated to sit for portraits or to be photographed, Einstein would occasionally do it to give a painter an opportunity to advance his career.)

Although this was technically a summer home, he stretched the season sometimes from the end of March to the beginning of November. One of his biographers said that Einstein loved this place so much that he even considered living there year-round.

One reason for his devotion to Caputh was that it was near the forest and had a beautiful view of the Havel, a large lake on which he sailed. His boat, the Tuemmler (German for something or somebody who sticks his nose into everything) was also built for him by some of his rich friends for his fiftieth birthday.

An amusing incident occurred once while Einstein was sailing in the Templiener See. At one point, a fellow physicist was also sailing with his young son, and his boat happened to come quite near to Einstein's. The other physicist said, "Look, there's Uncle Einstein's boat!" The boy looked and, seeing Einstein's shock of curly hair flying in the wind, asked, "Father, why is Uncle Einstein an aunt?"

Einstein's dining in Caputh was simple if there were no guests. For breakfast, he liked fried eggs and honey, which he procured fresh from local people. With this, he liked crisp rolls. He usually drank decaffeinated coffee (for medical reasons), which he brewed at the table with a small Sterno cooking device. For his large meal, taken at midday, he might have green beans and herring with cream sauce. He also liked new potatoes served with sour cream and butter. Asparagus, which was plentiful, was always on the table.

In the afternoon if there were guests, for tea Einstein would have small cookies and pound cake. Dinner was usually between 6:00 and 7:00 P.M. and consisted mainly of cold cuts, cheese, and more eggs. Einstein, who loved eggs and would have been unsympathetic to the modern strictures against cholesterol, normally ate at least three a day. Indeed, he could easily have been content with a diet of mushrooms and eggs.

But he also enjoyed salads, rice, and spaghetti, and would eat beef only if it was well done. If he was served meat that still showed traces of blood, he would growl, "Why am I given this? I am not a tiger!"

His friends the Tichmanns had a dog named Purcell that they left with the Einsteins each summer. Einstein was very fond of the dog, as the dog was of him. Purcell often accompanied Einstein on long walks in the forest and spent hours lying beside him on the terrace and once, when the Professor took an automobile ride to Potsdam, jumped in without anybody noticing. Purcell also co-existed well with the Einsteins' cat, Peter, who lived in Herta's bedroom.

Einstein lived totally spontaneously. As he did later at the Institute for Advanced Studies, he varied his routine at the Kaiser Wilhelm Institute, one day working there, another day working at home, another day not working at all. Some days he would stay in his bedroom all day, and other days he would go to the library or play his violin or piano for a few hours. For important journeys, he always had friends, such as Toni Mendel, who would lend him their automobiles, complete with chauffeurs.

Einstein, who also enjoyed going to a good movie, often traveling from Caputh to Potsdam to attend, had a social life that was quite active in the German days. He and his wife gave an average of two parties a month, many of them attended by such luminaries as Planck, Hauptmann, Mann, Chaplin, and Tagore. At these parties, Einstein's favorite drinks were a celery punch, mocha (which was a hot, strong coffee), and cognac. Otherwise, he hardly ever touched liquor, and Elsa kept all alcohol in a cabinet, as she did his Nobel Prize, in which Einstein seemed totally uninterested.

Three times each year, the Einsteins gave a major party. These were known as "Flicht," or "duty," parties, which reciprocated for all of the invitations that the Einsteins received during the year. The menu for these parties was usually fairly standard. They started with an egg-drop soup, followed by lox with egg mayonnaise. The main course would generally be a pork filet, which was followed by a dessert of strawberries with whipped cream, something that Einstein could eat several pounds of at a sitting.

But the pleasurable days of party-giving were soon over-shadowed by the growing cloud of Nazism. As anti-Semitism began to be officially sanctioned by the state, no Jew—no matter what his international reputation—was safe from State and state-sponsored harassment. The Einsteins began to see the handwriting on the wall. About the middle of April 1933 Einstein's step-daughter Margot and her husband, Dr. Dmitri Marianoff, fled to France. Shortly after that, one morning around six A.M. the police arrived at Einstein's apartment in Berlin. They searched all of the rooms and asked a lot of questions about Dr. Marianoff. One of the police stayed with Herta during the search, probably to prevent her from using the telephone.

A few months later, this time in the evening, another raid was made on the apartment by uniformed men. This time, they looked in every closet and every room and then collected all of the room, closet, and cabinet keys. The maid and Mrs. Rudolf Kayser (Ilsa) were then ushered into the library and given strict orders not to leave the room. After a long delay, the ladies finally ventured out of their imposed prison, only to find that the apartment had been plundered and the plunderers had gone. Carpets, pictures, a fur coat, and silver had been carted out. That evening, when Herta reported the thievery to the Berlin police, she received no cooperation whatsoever.

Gradually, Einstein realized that there was no alternative for him and his family but to leave Germany. They actually left the country prior to Hitler's accession to power, renouncing their German citizenship and driving the Nazis into a retaliatory frenzy. Refusing to accept his renunciation, they declared their intention to revoke his citizenship. Einstein later compared their folly to the Italians' public hanging of Mussolini after he had already been shot dead.

The Nazis proceeded to confiscate Einstein's bank account, loot his Caputh summer home, and hurl all of his writings, books, and papers onto bonfires in Berlin. Nazi-supporting professors were then enlisted to open an assault upon his theory of relativity, depicting Einstein as the arch-villain of a Jewish plot to pollute science and thereby wipe out civilization.

The harassment of Einstein and his family and friends continued for a long time after the professor had left Germany. Herta, the maid, received letters from the Einsteins—particularly from Margot—for years afterwards. But the correspondence always carried the censors' marks. Once, when Margot sent Herta a piece of jewelry from Paris, it arrived destroyed in a way that strongly suggested an act of intentional vandalism.

Several months after the Einsteins emigrated to the United States, Herta's parents were contacted by the police in an effort to find Herta's new address. Soon afterwards, Herta was summoned to appear at police headquarters where she noticed on the desk of the interviewing officer a sheaf of papers marked "Einstein," and she was questioned for a half-hour about her employers: Were they good to her? Did she continue to receive payments from them? The intent of the interrogator was obviously to extract incriminating evidence, but Herta remained imperturbable, rendering his efforts fruitless.

For Einstein, then, his original, youthful opinion of his homeland as a bastion of militarism and anti-Semitism had been upheld by the events of the early 1930's. But this time, unlike his earlier departure for Switzerland, he was to leave the land of his birth forever.

Shortly after his emigration, the Nazis put a price on Einstein's head—the equivalent of $50,000—and, demonstrating the moral debasement to which the country's leaders had sunk, published the fact in the German newspapers of the day. Einstein, in characteristic humility and humor, reportedly remarked, "I did not know that I was worth so much."

The stated intention of the Nazis to eliminate Einstein made his security a precarious matter. Before settling in the United States, he was shuffled into Holland and Belgium, where even his close friend, King Albert, couldn't guarantee his safety.

But Einstein was not totally forsaking his homeland and his people. He was still concerned not with just his own safety but with the safety of fellow Jews left behind under the Nazi brutality. An example of his solicitude appears in a letter written by Einstein to my father from Le Coq-Sur-Mer, Belgium, on 15 July 1933 and addressed to our residence at 45 East 85th Street in New York City:

Dear Mr. Bucky:

Thank you very much for the genuinely cordial and sympathetic words you addressed to me. The newspaper articles and actions which reveal hostility towards me do not impress me at all. However, I am very deeply concerned about the general decline and low level of culture which can be felt most keenly in Germany but which can also be generally observed in every part of the world.

I like your plan about organizing a Medical Mobile Team and I believe it is perfectly feasible. I hope that your idea will be successful.

You are wrong in assuming that I am in the center of the efforts revolving around the Organized Rescue Operations. I am living at a remote location and possess neither organizational talent nor connections to the relevant circles. Thanks to the confidence that people have in me, I am merely able to intervene in a few exceptional drastic cases.

I have been thinking carefully about your plan concerning a referral center abroad. If the German Government were to play with open cards, one could consider such a plan, although even then, the danger of corruption would be immense. But we are dealing with methods employing gangs who are able to go unpunished as they hit everybody and everything as they please, resorting to all kinds of pressure kept secret by terrorist means. I really do believe that any action aimed at keeping Jews in Germany would have the effect of speeding up their annihilation. You were probably able to reach this conclusion yourself with the help of information, material that can be easier obtained now thanks to better news reports. In this connection, I draw your attention particularly to the press agency, IMPRESS, in Paris, rue Mondetour 1. The distribution of this publication in foreign countries would be highly desirable (information of the American public and assistance of enterprises struggling to survive).

Cordially yours,

Albert Einstein

Einstein's final stop before America was England. It was during this English segment of his exile that, during a meeting with Stanley Baldwin, Einstein went into great detail concerning the growing danger of Hitler. He even predicted to Baldwin that Hitler, in a drive for world conquest, might force a new world war. Lord Baldwin responded to this by smiling and reassuringly touching Einstein's shoulder, saying, "Don't worry, Professor, we have our allies."

Einstein, of course, was soon to settle for the coming war in England's major ally—the United States of America.

2. Conversation: Thoughts on Germany and Hitler

BUCKY: The period of time after you left Germany must have been a trying one for you, Professor, what with the Nazi threats to your life following you around Europe.

EINSTEIN: Yes, of course. I don't ever recall in that era anyone else of a non-political stature having to be supplied with armed protection. I honestly did not like all the fuss, but everyone said that there was a price on my head. It was all really quite difficult. Do you know that while I was in Belgium—and remember that the King of Belgium, Albert, was my very dear friend—the police actually approached me to advise me to leave the country as they couldn't protect me from the Nazis?

BUCKY: Were you armed yourself during this time?

EINSTEIN: I wasn't, no, but my secretaries and the people around me were. It wasn't an easy time, no matter where we went, so I can assure you that I was glad to finally emigrate to the United

States, which was at least isolated from this special kind of madness.

BUCKY: To what extent do you feel that all Germans shared in the Nazi regime? Or do you think that Hitler was a Lone Ranger, so to speak, leading the innocent Germans into insanity?

EINSTEIN: I have mixed feelings on this. It can never be said that the German people can't be blamed for putting Hitler into power, because in this case, the unusual fact existed that Hitler's complete program was already published in his book, *Mein Kampf.* What more can a dictator do than to actually print his whole program before he executes it? And then, not only did the people put Hitler into power, but then they tolerated him for twelve years! On the other hand, I am of the opinion that a man like Hitler could not last for long with the German people and that he did cast a hypnotic spell on the people with his tremendous power of speech. And, also, he was able to manipulate the youth of Germany with the various Nazi youth organizations around the country.

BUCKY: I can't help but remember how, at the beginning of the war, you told me that it wouldn't surprise you in the least if after the Germans were defeated, the German people would claim that they were not really for Hitler but had been forced to support him because he was in control of the army. I doubted this, then, but it turned out to be true enough. During my wartime activities with the Office of Strategic Services, I operated the radio station Atlantic in England and my major job was to interview German prisoners of war. And do you know that seventy-five percent of them claimed, just as you said, that they were not really for Hitler and did not agree with him at all? It seems incomprehensible that intelligent people could make such disclaimers after their actions had been witnessed with horror by people all over the world.

EINSTEIN: Exactly. But this was predictable to me.

BUCKY: Of course, Hitler was only one example of totalitarian politics during this century. Centuries from now, the twentieth century is sure to be known as "the age of the dictators"— Hitler, Mao, Mussolini, Stalin, Franco, Salazar, to mention only a few. What are your thoughts on this phenomenon?

63

EINSTEIN: I detest regimentation. This is not to say that I am
opposed to an organization where one man is the brains and
the leader. Sometimes that is the only way that an organization
can fulfill its mission. But such organizations must be able to
elect such a man or repudiate him by election. Unfortunately,
there is a built-in danger in any organization or political division that the members or the electorate abdicate their respon-
sibilities to think and leave the burden of this to their leaders.
This is fine as long as the leader is upright and concerned only
for the good of the group. But if the leader departs from this
ideal, the danger develops of his turning into a dictator, such
as happened in Russia, Germany, and Italy. It isn't always the
philosophy that is at fault, but the men who are corrupted
with their power. For instance, the philosophy behind communism has a lot of merit, being concerned with ending the
exploitation of the common people and the sharing of goods
and labor according to needs and abilities. Communism as a
political theory is a tremendous experiment, but unfortunately, in Russia, it is an experiment conducted in a poorly
equipped laboratory.

BUCKY: Is regimentation the key to your hatred of totalitarianism,
or are there other factors that weigh as heavily?

EINSTEIN: Regimentation is an effect, not to say a cause, of totalitarianism. One of the *causes,* I believe, that leads to this is
that, generally, the functionaries who enforce the regimentation are men of low moral standards who, prior to their new
role, have never succeeded in accomplishing anything worth-
while in life. Suddenly, their new position of authority makes
them feel like a "somebody," and they revel in being able to
exert force upon their fellow citizens. This was particularly
noticeable in the Hitler regime where even those youths who
were often only fifteen or sixteen years old adopted a swagger-
ing pose when, as Hitler youth, they were permitted to carry
small arms weapons.

BUCKY: We saw how a madman like Hitler seduced a nation with
his flaming oratory, but how do you explain the sway of totalitarianism in countries where the leaders were less, shall we
say, charismatic—for instance, Franco in Spain?

EINSTEIN: I think that the biggest weapon of the totalitarian states is the oppression of the individual by economic means. In this manner, the people are made to fall in line with the principles of the governments in general.

BUCKY: With all that we have witnessed in this century, so far, what do you see for the future of the world and, particularly, for the subjugated nations?

EINSTEIN: That is very difficult to say. I think that the pillars of civilized human existence have been weakened tremendously in the last thirty years. The most disturbing thing is that countries that previously had a high standard of morality and that always recognized the rights of human beings have indirectly admitted that the truth for its own sake has no justification—indeed, does not even have to be tolerated. Suddenly, arbitrary rule, oppression, and even religious persecution and atrocities are accepted as justifiable and unavoidable. I frankly don't understand how people who work for and support these regimes can live with their own consciences. Surely, they must know that not only are their actions unjust, but criminal toward the individual and, collectively, to humanity. But of course, like nature, which is impervious to the destruction it sometimes reaps, people become accustomed to just about anything in life, closing their eyes to the evil around them. As for the future, one can only hope, as in the history of the world, that the will for justice and truth practiced by individuals and leaders has done more for human beings than all the shrewd, trouble-making politicians. Moses, after all, was a better man than Machiavelli. Perhaps it is this will that might triumph in the end over the forces of darkness.

CHAPTER FOUR

Fateful Summer

1. Secretive Summer at Peconic Bay

One of the greatest ironies of history centers on the fact that one of the gentlest of men, Albert Einstein, was instrumental in the development of the greatest destructive force ever unleashed upon mankind: the atomic bomb. Indeed, the irony is doubly curious when we reflect upon the fact that he was one of the most visible and well-known pacifists of all time.

Einstein's peaceful intent embraced even the animal world. Although he was not a vegetarian, he was adamantly opposed to the killing of animals except for food. Indeed, I can even recall many muggy summer evenings when Einstein would menacingly brandish a fly swatter. But, unlike most of us, Einstein would never use it to kill the flies disturbing his summer serenity but would only swish it around to chase off the intruders. Of him it could truly be said, "He wouldn't hurt a fly."

If Einstein hated anything more than physical violence, it was German militarism. His life had been a running battle against the Prussian streak that ran through German history like bad blood. Twice he had left Germany because of it: once to pursue his career in Switzerland; the last time to flee those in Nazi Germany who had put a price on his head because of his Jewishness.

Einstein recognized that in Hitler, Germany had reached the zenith of its militancy. And it was for this reason—and only this reason—that this great pacifist temporarily forsook his philosophy to help the Western allies get the atomic bomb before the Germans.

Thus it was in the summer of 1939, while the Einsteins and our family were enjoying one of our idyllic summers in Peconic Bay in eastern Long Island, that Einstein became swept up in a storm of meetings and secret correspondence that would inevitably result in the Manhattan Project.

Peconic Bay (which is now called "Cutchogue," located at Nassau Point) was one of Einstein's favorite spots. Indeed, we spent two summers there—1938 and 1939—thanks to Einstein's love of sailing (he once called Little Peconic Bay "the most beautiful sailing ground I ever experienced").

As usual on our summer vacations, Einstein kept pretty much to himself, opting to spend as much time as possible sailing and reserving the rest of his time for walks in the woods with our family, as well as, of course, thinking.

One friend that I recall Einstein making in Peconic Bay was David Rothman, who owned a department store in nearby Southold. This friendship arose from an innocent visit to the store by Einstein's step-daughter Margot to buy a sculptor's chisel. When Margot discovered in conversation that Rothman was an amateur violinist, a meeting was arranged with Einstein and the two became fast friends.

I recall the two playing duets on the violin and Einstein obviously surpassing the storeowner in virtuosity. Realizing this, Rothman was responsible for putting Einstein in touch with several other better string players so that the group could indulge in Einstein's second favorite pastime (next to sailing)—playing string quartets. By the way, the store in question is still, fifty years later, in Southold, now run by Rothman's son Robert.

Our house in Peconic was on Old Cove Road (along with the town's change of name, this street's name has also been changed, to West Cove Road). Interestingly when, as a result of visits from the physicists Leo Szilard, Eugene Wigner, and Edward Teller to Peconic, Einstein addressed his famous letter to President Roosevelt, he absent mindedly wrote his return address as "Old *Grove* Road." One journalist has recently recorded how a Belgian student seeking research assistance actually wrote to "The House of Albert Einstein, Old Grove Road" fifty years later!

When, because of Margot's need for drier air, we decided to switch our vacation spot in 1940 to Saranac Lake in the Adirondacks, Einstein eschewed his favored Peconic Bay with regrets that he expressed in letters to his friend Rothman. Writing from

Saranac, he said, "I feel very unhappy that I am not able to this year spend the summer near your beautiful place in Long Island. The health of my daughter compels me to go to the Adirondacks. . . . Meanwhile, great decisions are being made on the other side of the water. One is always between hope and fear, in my case hope prevails."

Later in the summer, he again wrote to Rothman, saying, "I am going sailing daily with my sister and I am homesick when I think of the beautiful musical evenings."

We returned to Saranac Lake in the summer of 1941, and Einstein again wrote fondly to Rothman, who had just sent the physicist a pair of sandals as a gift: "It was very kind of you to send me again this year a pair of my favorite sandals. I cannot wear them yet because those you have given me last year are still of kingly elegance. I wear them always, in the sailboat and out."

But back to the summer of '39, when the peace and tranquility of Einstein's sailing in Peconic Bay were jarred by the famous physicists Szilard and Wigner, who called him at our summer residence to request an urgent meeting.

His first meeting with them took place in the middle of July 1939—historians place the date as July 15—when both physicists drove to Long Island, becoming lost in the process (the story goes that hopes for this famous meeting had almost been abandoned when the two men came upon a small boy who was able to lead them to our cabin). It is a tribute to Einstein's integrity that even though our family and he were the closest of friends and spent that entire summer together, he never divulged the purpose of this or subsequent meetings. But their import was indicated by the obvious weight that he seemed to carry on his shoulders for the rest of that summer.

In hindsight, it is understandable that Einstein should have turned so reflective and somber after Szilard and Wigner—and, later, Edward Teller—visited. For, of course, they had come to advise him of the news that the expatriate German physicist Lise Meitner had relayed to Western scientists of the successful atomic chain reaction achieved by Otto Hahn in Germany at the Kaiser Wilhelm Institute. To knowledgeable physicists, this pivotal event signaled the dawn of a new and dangerous era for mankind. The more immediate danger was that this discovery had been made inside the Third Reich.

Unfortunately, civilian government leaders lacked the expertise to reach the same sort of conclusion. Hahn's epic achievement was likely to go unnoticed in nonscientific circles, leaving Hitler able to exploit the work of his physicists in his manic quest for power and Lebensraum that was soon to run amok throughout Europe.

Consequently, the visits to Peconic Bay became occasions for the quartet of physicists to consider their options. These included among others, avoiding the United States government, since bureaucratic red tape was seen as an obstacle to speedy research; Einstein writing to a friend in the Belgian Cabinet (vetoed by the group as a breach of protocol, the equivalent of dealing with a foreign government without first getting clearance from the State Department); or seeking government financing for private research at Columbia University, where Szilard worked.

Finally, thanks to a coincidental introduction to an economist and banker—who happened to be a friend and advisor to President Roosevelt—it was decided that a letter would be drafted, signed by Einstein, and delivered personally to the President by Alexander Sachs, an economist who was one of his close friends. The letter went through several drafts, with input from Einstein, Szilard, and Sachs himself. The final version was signed by Einstein on 2 August 1939. Sachs did not get a chance to deliver the letter until over two months later, but the delay, until after Hitler's September invasion of Poland, may have helped to highlight its urgency.

Einstein's instincts concerning the flow of history had usually been correct. Early in the 1930's, when there was not even a hint of an atomic bomb, he had discussed with me his fear that if the world did not soon come to its senses on disarmament, many nations could face destruction. This he based upon the increasing efficiency of the airplane since World War I and the development of greater accuracy in bombing.

Later, after the atomic bomb had been developed, Einstein said he was quite sure that it would not remain a secret known only by the United States and Britain for long. History, of course, soon proved him right.

His influence on atomic bomb research was of a secondary nature. He was instrumental, via his famous letter to Roosevelt, in the President's decision to set up the Briggs Advisory Committee on Uranium, which consisted of several of the nation's top scientists. He wrote a second letter about five months later (addressed to Sachs, but for FDR's eyes), outlining what was known about the state of German research. But after this, Einstein was not called upon again for about two years. At that time, he was dealing with a new crowd of political functionaries who knew nothing of his earlier role in prodding Roosevelt. Ironically, these people decided that, because of Einstein's pacifist background, he was too much of a security risk to be trusted with details of current research.

And so Einstein, aside from assisting the Navy in attempting to figure out the laws that governed detonation waves, was kept in the dark for the duration of the Manhattan Project. (I often accompanied Einstein to his meetings with naval officers in my own capacity as an officer of the Office of Strategic Services, and I once told him jokingly: "Well, you are so involved with the Navy now that you might as well wear a Navy uniform." Einstein, a man for whom uniforms were anathema, was so amused that he broke into one of his loud, staccato laughs.) Indeed, the day the first atomic bomb was dropped on Hiroshima, Einstein learned of the event like many other Americans from a news report. As he came downstairs for an afternoon snack, Helen Dukas informed him of the blast, and Einstein sadly murmured, "Oh weh," meaning "Alas."

Prior to the development of the bomb, Einstein had felt that to ignore the potential of nuclear chain reactions could be suicide for the Allies. All known information seemed to point to the fact that the German scientists, working in the Kaiser Wilhelm Institute and in other places such as Peenemunde were in a race to put the secrets of chain reaction to practical wartime use. Foremost in raising these suspicions was the fact that Germany had clamped a moratorium on the export of uranium from lands occupied by the Reich and was frantically attempting to produce heavy water in newly conquered Norway.

For these reasons, Einstein felt that the Allies had to follow their natural instinct for self-preservation by trying to win the race for this deadly discovery.

It is ironic, in a way, that subsequent events proved the race for the atomic bomb to have been, in retrospect, unnecessary. The German research effort was hampered by many problems that caused it to die a-borning after reaching a plateau in 1942 that placed it ahead of the Allies' progress.

Many theories have been ventured as to why German research stalled. Perhaps significant was the fact that the research on atomic fission and its practical conversion to destructive power was placed under the leadership of the scientists in Germany. In contrast, the Americans' Manhattan Project was directed by the military under Gen. Leslie R. Groves. Scientists, by nature, are a slow, plodding lot who are painstaking in their experimentation. That characteristic does not lend itself to timetables. In comparison, Groves may have rubbed many scientists the wrong way by his militaristic approach, but he set deadlines, demanded results, and brooked no excuses. As one author has put it: "In short, the behavior of the German scientific leaders demonstrated that during war, science cannot be safely left to the scientists."

Another aspect in the Germans' failure to produce a bomb was the personality of the leader of the effort, Dr. Walter Gerlach. Gerlach was known to be a lazy person and some of his decisions were, in retrospect, questionable, such as permitting two different research groups to compete for the necessary materials to build uranium piles.

Still another reason often cited for this failure was the lack of any real commitment on the part of Hitler and his henchmen to the idea of an atomic bomb. This was due, in part, to Hitler's cockiness following his easy marches through Poland, Belgium, France, the Low Countries, and Eastern Europe. With such conventional military successes achieved with such ease, who needed an expensive super-weapon?

But I have theorized from my own readings on the subject and from many conversations that I had at the time with Einstein, a different, and perhaps surprising, reason for Germany's inability to successfully create an atomic bomb. It is a theory that was buttressed several years ago when, at a scientific exhibit in New Orleans, I met and had a significant conversation with Dr. Kurt Sauerwein, who at the time was chairman of Isotopen-Technik, a company in Haan, West Germany, that is one of his country's largest producers of isotopes. Before World War II, Dr. Sauerwein had been a researcher at the Kaiser Wilhelm Institute, where Otto Hahn was undertaking his research.

Dr. Sauerwein told me that, when Hahn called a meeting of fellow physicists to inform them of his successful chain reaction, he insisted that those attending the meeting sign a statement promising that they would do nothing to allow this new and startling information to fall into the hands of the "mad dog Hitler." Dr. Sauerwein said that most of the scientists at the Institute who were privy to this information did indeed band together secretly out of fear of what might happen if this information should fall into Hitler's hands.

From that time on, according to Sauerwein, while paying lip service to the stated goals of turning the nuclear knowledge into a military mega-weapon, the scientists dragged their feet, engaging in a "conspiracy of peace."

Such a reason for Germany's falling short in this race with the Allies has been hinted at in the past. For instance, an Allied analysis of the German research written in 1945 stated: "German science was not without guile, and took advantage of the lack of understanding of science by those in authority to engage in interesting scientific research, under the guise of war-work, that could not possibly help the war effort."

One of the bomb researchers, Dr. Werner Heisenberg, wrote in a letter to an expatriate physicist, Dr. Hans Bethe: "German physicists had no desire to make atomic bombs, and were glad to be spared the decision by force of external circumstances."

In keeping with this train of thought, Dr. Gerlach had no compunction about diverting funds earmarked for nuclear research to further other scientific objectives. The historian David Irving has suggested that, while the Reich had propagated the slogan, "German science in the cause of war," to Gerlach the slogan might just as well have been, "The war in the cause of German science."

Buttressing Dr. Sauerwein's observations are such comments as that of Dr. Carl-Friedrich von Weizsacker, one of the leaders of the research effort, who after the war, while in detention, said; "I believe the reason why we didn't do it was that all the physicists didn't want to do it, on principle."

Having been present at many of Einstein's conversations about this crucial matter, I realize now that this was, indeed, the case, and enough evidence exists to support this. For example, it is part of the historical record that one of the researchers, a Professor Esau, advised a liaison officer from the German Admiralty, a Professor Haxel, that Hitler should not be apprised of the possibilities of a uranium bomb, lest he incarcerate all scientists until the project was completed. Esau suggested that Haxel describe the research project as an attempt to create a "uranium engine."

Another curious sidelight was the "incident of the erroneous invitations." At a meeting of the Reich Research Council slated for 26 February 1942, many of the researchers were scheduled to divulge in eight brief, nontechnical talks, much of the secret work they had done. A secretary was supposed to send invitations out to many of the Reich's high command luring them to the meeting with the prospect of explanations of highly complex subjects. But, for some unexplained reason, this secretary instead sent invitations outlining highly technical scientific papers that were to be read at a related conference. The invitations proved to be off-putting, the high command unanimously made their excuses to avoid the conference, and this obscure secretary—by mistake or by guile?—may have altered the war's course by keeping these important leaders in the dark.

Never underestimate the capacity of the human spirit to combat tyranny and evil, no matter how strongly it may enchain. I am convinced, more so after my chance meeting with Dr. Sauerwein, who has since died, that German physicists willingly cooled their heels in their enforced efforts to create a super-bomb that could be used to devastate Hitler's enemies. Einstein himself, in a conversation with me about this episode, alluded to this as well, saying that Szilard had informed him of the attitudes of the physicists.

This only added to a certain depression that Einstein felt over his urgings to Roosevelt to try to beat the Germans to the atomic punch, particularly after the United States ended up using the bombs in attacks on Hiroshima and Nagasaki.

Speaking with Linus Pauling, Einstein later said, "I may have made one great mistake in my life when I signed the letter to President Roosevelt." This, of course, was said in the luxury of hindsight. Nevertheless, he was quite depressed and often told his friends that, had he known that the Germans would fail in their mission to develop the bomb, he would never have taken the role he did in promoting it for the United States.

It was actually only when my father was able to convince Einstein of the importance of isotopes—a by-product of the bomb—in modern medicine, that Einstein's depression subsided. The sword, indeed, had double edges, as it turned out, and if he despised its destructive thrust, he knew that it could at least be turned over to help cure mankind's ills.

2. Conversation: Thoughts on War and the Atomic Bomb

BUCKY: Dr. Einstein, your reputation is sealed in the history books as a pacifist. But if you were so staunch a pacifist, how could you honestly account for your interest in the development of the atomic bomb?

EINSTEIN: From the moment that I set foot in the United States when I emigrated, I began to change my mind. I soon decided that to be absolutely passive with a dictator like Hitler would be sheer suicide for humanity. I did not come to my position thoughtlessly. Only after I had satisfied myself fully that experiments in Germany had already succeeded in producing satisfactory atomic fission did I decide to cooperate with this work. What really got me worried was one authentic report that the minute Germany took over Czechoslovakia, they immediately stopped the sale of uranium from the Czech mines.

BUCKY: Have you ever had a guilty conscience over the work that you did in furthering the bomb, because of the great suffering it brought to so many human beings in Japan?

EINSTEIN: No, I have no reason to have a bad conscience about this because when I worked on these things, it was my honest conviction and intention to do it for the good of humanity and not for their destruction. But that does not mean that I do not feel sad that the things which I gave them had been used for destruction instead of for the benefit of mankind.

BUCKY: Of course, your pioneer work that led to the bomb also had some interesting side benefits in the medical area.

EINSTEIN: That is true, and that pleases me. I wished first that this benefit could be put to the use first of helping those thousands of Japanese who suffered from the terrible effects of radioactivity. But, of course, there are other benefits as well. I think that atomic power will eventually have many uses in industry, and I think that in the not-too-distant future, atomic energy will replace ordinary fuels for engines, for example, in ships and airplanes. The main advantage of this would be that the volume of fuel needed in comparison to today's standards would guarantee a much longer operating time for the engines.

BUCKY: Once the German threat was squelched, and the Allies were successful, you reverted to your dedication to pacifism. How did you arrive at your pacifistic philosophy?

EINSTEIN: It was completely instinctive to me, simply because the murder of men is repulsive to me. And let me state unequivocably that I see absolutely no difference whether one commits a murder in civilian life or during the war. My attitude of pacifism, thus, did not stem from any intellectual theory but was based on my antipathy to every kind of cruelty and hatred. I believe strongly that one of the main factors in the moral decay of humanity is the existence of wars. Even countries that are highly respected will openly submit to tyrants during wartime under camouflage of the old saying that "might makes right." This is the real evil of humanity which we must all realize and fight to erase with all of our energies.

BUCKY: Given the natural instincts of governments, do you really think that it is possible to attain your dream of a warless world?

EINSTEIN: First, let me state to you that the practicability or impracticability of our goal does not detract from the ideal. Wars have no aim except for material advantages. There is not the slightest bit of morality innate in any war. But to answer your question, I think that there are some options available, most of which center around re-education. If the minds of the people are prepared properly, I think that a satisfactory solution could be found. We must foster good will among peoples. Treaties are not the answer. They can too easily be broken, after all. Another important element of attaining a peaceful world is for the people of the world to be educated in the arts. Once people become artistically aware, nationalism takes on a lesser significance. It is impossible to despise an artist from another country just because that country's government takes on differing political views.

BUCKY: Do you think that it is important for nationalism to be totally expunged in order to eliminate war?

EINSTEIN: Absolutely. The first thing that must be done is to eliminate import and export duties on merchandise between countries. This is one of the biggest obstacles to peace. This could go a long way to eliminating selfishness in international relations. I remember an incident many years ago that illustrates this idea. It was during Roosevelt's administration, and I was talking with an American diplomat about the Japanese problem. I remember asking him why the American government does not just boycott Japan in order to avert the improper traffic of munitions. The diplomat objected, saying that there were too many American interests in Japan, making it unfeasible to take action of that type.

BUCKY: But wouldn't eliminating tariffs only reinforce selfishness when unrestricted imports, for instance, forced people out of work in some instances?

EINSTEIN: This is only part of the solution, of course. In conjunction with this, I think that we must work towards a system of world government. In this way, the elimination of tariffs would work just as the federal system of the United States works. After all, New York does not feel it necessary to war upon New Jersey. Why, then, should Germany war upon France when they are all part of the same system.

BUCKY: It just seems that, as nice as it sounds, world government is impossible. It seems that man's natural instinct for self-preservation, along with his natural jealousy and his longing for individual power are all qualities that can never be erased from the world.

EINSTEIN: It is difficult, I admit, but not impossible. These evils of which you speak would be overshadowed through a proper world government which would clearly educate people on how they would benefit from such an arrangement. I can only compare such an arrangement to the basic concept of a happy marriage, the primary function of which is a mutual understanding of each other's problems and the ability to give and take gracefully. In the end, both partners of a happy marriage arrive at greater benefits than they could ever have arrived at as individuals. Well, the idea of a world government is nothing more than the proper marriages of governments among themselves—a communal marriage, if you will.

BUCKY: But there are divorces among marriages. Do you not think that there might be "divorces" among countries that might lead to more war?

EINSTEIN: The key word in this thing is "proper" marriages. Proper marriages do not lead to divorces. Those who would administer a world government must do so with a great deal of wisdom and foresight. As for wars, this question leads to the third aspect of achieving lasting peace. First, we eliminate tariffs; secondly, we institute a world government. Finally, we must work on achieving total disarmament. This could be done in a couple of stages. First, all nations could turn over all of their armaments to an impartial international organization, which would hold them in escrow. While they were being held, honest and sincere negotiations would be initiated by the people's representatives. It would be important for all people to express their views on the issue. One of the major faults of humanity is that they do not have the courage to speak out for fear of having reprisals taken against them, for instance, by their employers. But, really, the common man does not have anything to fear because the majority of his fellow men agree with him on what is right and what is wrong. It would be important, also, for a special type of organization to be formed, consisting of respected leaders from various fields, who would propagandize the masses on the evils of war. These leaders would use all religious means to associate these ideas to make them as understandable as possible to the broad masses. Once the people were properly educated, then their representatives could easily negotiate a disarmament plan and the arms being held in escrow could then be destroyed.

BUCKY: It would seem to me that such a disarmament would have to be much more gradual than you indicate in order to be successful.

EINSTEIN: I don't think so. As far as I'm concerned, a gradual disarmament plan is a dishonest plan. After all, if people are willing to abolish wars by disarming, why should they not disarm completely and immediately? The only reason people could have for doing this gradually would be that they have suspicions that the abolition of war would not work as a peaceful solution. Thus, they would not want to be caught short-handed, so to speak, in case of a breakdown in communications between countries. I don't want to give the wrong impression that I am somehow unaware of realities. It would be suicide, after all, for a peaceful nation to disarm knowing that its enemies have not the slightest intention of doing so. The only way that this can succeed is if all nations would abide by the basic principles of complete disarmament and cooperation.

BUCKY: Don't you think perhaps that with the advent of atomic weapons, the concept of a "balance of terror" might serve as a deterrent to war? I can never forget how, after World War II, when I served with the Office of Strategic Services in England, I personally witnessed every poison gas container that the allies had being dumped into the ocean without ever being used. Both sides had it, but both realized the danger of this gas to mankind in general, so that it was never used.

EINSTEIN: I can't agree that you can depend upon this to work. Any buildup of arms is a potential danger, if only because many times the people that control this power become over-confident and begin to take actions that directly or indirectly can lead to wars. I agree with you that the atomic bomb, in the sense that you speak, could be a peacemaker among nations.

However, we mustn't forget the lesson of Hitler. One never knows when a fool might trigger an explosion.

BUCKY: Well, in that case, the so-called hot-lines between countries would be able to resolve this problem.

EINSTEIN: This might be logical and we could only hope that if it should ever go that far, people would come to their senses before it was too late. The success of this program for disarmament depends upon the cooperation of common interests between countries. This is the ultimate and greatest asset for permanent peace. Only when countries have common ideals and understanding can a harmony of this type be created and preserved.

CHAPTER FIVE

Einstein and Religion

1. Conflicts in Religion

One of the ironies of Einstein's life on two continents was that his Jewishness was a continual factor in his experiences, both negative and positive, and yet Einstein never considered himself a Jew in any conventional sense.

Looking back over his seventy-five years, we see his religion affecting him in many different circumstances. For example, his first leave-taking of Germany early in the century was, in part, due to that country's increasing public anti-Semitism. There were his on-going communications with the leaders of the Zionist movement to establish a Jewish homeland. And, of course, his ultimate flight from Nazi Germany because of his perceived Jewishness. Finally, there was even the offer of the premiership of Israel that was made by its representatives—not once, but twice. All of these facts might easily lead one to imagine a man of great religious conviction and discipline.

But those who knew him well knew that this was far from the case. For Einstein continually played down his Jewishness—not for safety, as one might very well have done in the climate of fear of 1930s Germany—but out of a genuine sense of universality, a common bond that Einstein felt with all of mankind.

All of Einstein's informal discussions with me were emblematic of this sense of universality. He felt very strongly that all religions came from the same source and that from those religions came man's drive to create the splendors of the arts and sciences.

What was that source? Well, Einstein firmly believed that primitive man's original reason for religion was to overcome fear. His fears were of hunger, wild beasts, the elements, sickness, and death. Einstein called this "the religion of fear."

But Einstein's religious beliefs really encompassed a broader scope—a system of beliefs long understood as "cosmic religion." This religious concept was connected with the wonders of nature and of the universe and posited a man who was an integral part of the cosmos, something very different from the traditional religious concepts of the Judeo-Christian heritage, which counter-balance the temporal with the spiritual. Einstein clung to this religious philosophy for many years and his espousal of it was deemed important enough to warrant a rebuttal from the Catholic polemicist and orator Bishop Fulton J. Sheen, who, discussing Einstein's "cosmic religion," quipped: "Who ever wanted to die for the Milky Way?"

On the more down-to-earth level, Einstein's philosophy might be easily equated to what is today called ethical humanism. In other words, he believed that the way a man behaves in daily life should be based upon logic, truth, a mature ethical sense, sympathy, and general social needs. To act ethically, in other words, is to lead a religious life. This, coupled with a cosmic religious feeling, was for Einstein the strongest and noblest motive for any type of scientific research.

This, therefore, is somewhat removed from his official standing as a Jew. My father told me many times that Einstein was not a very religious person in the traditional sense and even went so far as to say that Einstein had told him he didn't believe in God. Yet, this does not exactly square with my own perceptions of Einstein's beliefs. The professor had told me that his own father was not very religious, and that perhaps that was the initial impetus that drove Einstein to a wider, more universalistic concept. Even so, he still composed a number of songs to honor God, which I heard him sing to himself many times. I also heard him say that anybody who loves nature must love God. He also told me once that ideas, as such, stem from God. This disparity with his earlier statements to my father might have something to do with the fact that he was an older man when I had the opportunity to converse with him in depth. His views by then may have mellowed.

As far as the omnipresent clash between science and religion is concerned, Einstein could see no problem with their co-existence. In his view, the universe was a creation of God, and within

81

that creation was the wonder of the mind of man. That mind had been created with the ability to imagine and work out all manner of new concepts and discoveries. Whatever that mind could generate through the centuries was all in keeping with universal law, since Einstein could not envision a God who would intentionally confuse by paradox and contradictions.

Also at cross purposes with the Judaic tradition was Einstein's conception of God. In the Judaic tradition, as in the Christian religion that stemmed from it, even within the Catholic trinity God is envisioned as a singular concept.

But Einstein told me many times that he did not believe in a single God. He said he could not imagine how God could manifest himself in a human countenance. Rather, he believed that there was a cosmic force that could develop things that mortal men could not even begin to comprehend. From this higher, cosmic, consciousness in Einstein's view, stems all of the wonders of the universe.

So, all in all, Einstein's religious life diverged significantly from those of ordinary adherents of the Jewish faith. But then, again, Einstein was no ordinary person. I recall his telling me that, during his earlier years, when he would apply for various positions and come to a column asking for details about his religion, he would mark down "dissident," thus demonstrating his disinterest in any one faith.

He once also said that, were he not a Jew, he would probably have chosen to be a Quaker. This I could visualize quite easily, for Einstein, in his daily life, evinced that special gentleness that has always been synonymous with the Society of Friends.

During an interview with Professor William Hermanns, Einstein once said that he could never accept any conceptualization of God that was based upon fear, either fear of life or fear of death, or one that required a blind belief, totally removed from logic. Nor did he envision God in any personal sense. In that respect, he said that if he were to talk about a personal God, he would consider himself to be a liar.

But he wasn't a Quaker. And despite all of his intellectual quibbles with religious principles, Einstein's life remained bound up with his Judaistic heritage. Even though he didn't feel strongly about religion, he still felt bound to support Zionist causes, perhaps as a hedge against the sort of mindless slaughter that took the lives of so many of his brothers in Europe during the Second World War.

But as far as the little daily observances of religion were concerned, Einstein was practically uninvolved. In fact, when he lived in Berlin and Orthodox Jews would visit his home, they would only take tea, since they knew that there was no kosher food to be had there. There is an anecdote in this vein about a time when a stranger stopped Einstein on the street and asked him where he might find a kosher restaurant. Einstein mentioned a particular place and gave the man the proper directions. Not quite satisfied, the man badgered Einstein, saying, "You're sure that this is a kosher restaurant?" At this, Einstein laughed and answered, "Yes, it is. But only the bull is kosher because he only eats grass."

Though Einstein was not totally in tune with his Jewishness, I think that the sorrowful events of the first half of the century led him as he reached his later years to feel more and more of a bond with his fellow Jews.

Anti-Semitism began rearing its head early in his life. At the Luitpold Gymnasium, Einstein early felt what it was like to be on the receiving end of this ugly prejudice. He often remembered the religious classes in that school, populated mostly by Catholics, in which the teacher would go to the needless trouble of demonstrating with a nail how Christ was crucified. Of course, as one of the few Jews in those classes, Einstein suffered the prejudicial wrath of his fellow students, bearing the burden of guilt that Jews were forced to endure until the Second Vatican Council officially repudiated a doctrine of mass guilt.

But anti-Semitism marched onward, particularly in his native land, and not even a man of Einstein's reputation could escape its consequences. He had the distinction of having a street named for him in his hometown, then having the Nazis change its name as a personal insult, only to have it changed back to honor him after World War II. (In fact, when Einstein died, this street in Ulm was widened by thirty-six feet to make it into a major thoroughfare.) But the hurt had been done. Even when Ulm wanted to make him an honorary citizen after the war, he could not forget and bury his bitter feelings. He refused the honor.

But the suffering had not been in vain, in Einstein's view. He felt that the Jews who died in Hitler's pogroms had strengthened the bond uniting all of the Jews in the world. He further believed that those same sacrifices should lead the Jews, as well as everyone else, to work toward a goal of achieving a better and more humane society.

Einstein's work behind the scenes for the Zionist cause had not been forgotten, either. One day, in 1948, the telephone rang in his Princeton home and when Helen Dukas answered and heard that Washington was on the line, she said, beckoning to Einstein: "What happened now?" But it was the Israeli Ambassador to the United States, Abba Eban, calling to ask Einstein informally whether he would accept the premiership of Israel. Perhaps he felt like Paderewski, the great concert pianist and Premier of Poland who, when he walked up the steps at Versailles during the great conference of 1919, was greeted by the British Prime Minister, Lloyd George, with these words: "Ah, Paderewski, the greatest pianist in the world! Paderewski, the Premier of Poland! Mon Dieu, what a comedown!" Well, Einstein, the greatest scientist in the world, was impressed by the offer, but he refused. Smiling, he told Abba Eban, "I know a little bit about nature but hardly anything about human beings."

Israel was persistent, though. Again, in 1952, he was asked more formally by Chaim Weizmann to accept the premiership. This time, Einstein wrote his refusal in simple, but eloquent terms: "All my life I have dealt with objective matters, hence I lack both the natural aptitude and experience to deal properly with people and to exercise official functions. For these reasons alone, I should be unsuited to fulfill the duties of the high office, even if advancing age was not making increasing inroads on my strength."

So there we have Einstein's life in religion, a constant balance between the inquisitiveness that was his very nature and the bonding that was, perhaps, his heritage. Perhaps his religious philosophy was best summed up in the answer he gave an interviewer once when he was asked what one can believe in this world.

"I believe," he said, "in the brotherhood of mankind and the individualism of the single person. But if you want me to prove to you that what I believe is true, this I cannot do."

2. *Conversation: Thoughts on Religion and Anti-Semitism*

BUCKY: It's ironic that your name has been synonymous with science in the twentieth century, and yet there has always been a lot of controversy surrounding you in relation to religious questions. How do you account for this unusual circumstance, since science and religion are usually thought to be at odds?

EINSTEIN: Well, I do not think that it is necessarily the case that science and religion are natural opposites. In fact, I think that there is a very close connection between the two. Further, I think that science without religion is lame and, conversely, that religion without science is blind. Both are important and should work hand-in-hand. It seems to me that whoever doesn't wonder about the truth in religion and in science might as well be dead.

BUCKY: So then, you consider yourself to be a religious man?

EINSTEIN: I believe in mystery and, frankly, I sometimes face this mystery with great fear. In other words, I think that there are many things in the universe that we cannot perceive or penetrate and that also we experience some of the most beautiful things in life in only a very primitive form. Only in relation to these mysteries do I consider myself to be a religious man. But I sense these things deeply. What I cannot understand is how there could possibly be a God who would reward or punish his subjects or who could induce us to develop our will in our daily life.

BUCKY: You don't believe in God, then?

EINSTEIN: Ah, this is what I mean about religion and science going hand-in-hand! Each has a place, but each must be relegated to its sphere. Let's assume that we are dealing with a theoretical physicist or scientist who is very well-acquainted with the different laws of the universe, such as how the planets orbit the sun and how the satellites in turn orbit around their respective planets. Now, this man who has studied and understands these different laws—how could he possibly believe in one God

85

who would be capable of disturbing the paths of these great orbiting masses?

No, the natural laws of science have not only been worked out theoretically but have been proven also in practice. I cannot then believe in this concept of an anthropomorphic God who has the powers of interfering with these natural laws. As I said before, the most beautiful and most profound religious emotion that we can experience is the sensation of the mystical. And this mysticality is the power of all true science. If there is any such concept as a God, it is a subtle spirit, not an image of a man that so many have fixed in their minds. In essence, my religion consists of a humble admiration for this illimitable superior spirit that reveals itself in the slight details that we are able to perceive with our frail and feeble minds.

BUCKY: Do you think perhaps that most people need religion to keep them in check, so to speak?

EINSTEIN: No, clearly not. I do not believe that a man should be restrained in his daily actions by being afraid of punishment after death or that he should do things only because in this way he will be rewarded after he dies. This does not make sense. The proper guidance during the life of a man should be the weight that he puts upon ethics and the amount of consideration that he has for others. Education has a great role to play in this respect. Religion should have nothing to do with a fear of living or a fear of death, but should instead be a striving after rational knowledge.

BUCKY: And yet, with all of these thoughts, you are still identified strongly in the public mind as definitely Jewish and this certainly is a very traditional religion.

EINSTEIN: Actually, my first religious training of any kind was in the Catholic catechism. A fluke, of course, only because the primary school that I first went to was a Catholic one. I was, as a matter of fact, the only Jewish child in the school. This actually worked to my advantage, since it made it easier for me to isolate myself from the rest of the class and find that comfort in solitude that I so cherished.

BUCKY: But don't you find any discrepancy between your previous somewhat anti-religious statements and your willingness to be identified publicly as a Jew?

EINSTEIN: Not necessarily. Actually it is a very difficult thing to even define a Jew. The closest that I can come to describing it is to ask you to visualize a snail. A snail that you see at the ocean consists of the body that is snuggled inside of the house which it always carries around with it. But let's picture what would happen if we lifted the shell off of the snail. Would we not still describe the unprotected body as a snail? In just the same way, a Jew who sheds his faith along the way, or who even picks up a different one, is still a Jew.

BUCKY: You were the focus of much attack on the part of the Nazis in Germany because of your Jewishness. What explanation have you come up with for why the Jews have been hated so much throughout history?

EINSTEIN: It seems obvious to me that Jews make an ideal scapegoat for any country experiencing social, economic, or political difficulties. The reason for this is twofold. First of all, there is hardly a country in the world that does not have a Jewish segment in the population. And secondly, wherever Jews reside, they are a minority of the population, and a small minority at that, so that they are not powerful enough to defend themselves against a mass attack. It is very easy for governments to divert attention from their own mistakes by blaming Jews for this or that political theory, such as communism or socialism.

For instance, after the First World War, many Germans accused the Jews first of starting the war and then of losing it. This is nothing new, of course. Throughout history, Jews have been accused of all sorts of treachery, such as poisoning water wells or murdering children as religious sacrifices. Much of this can be attributed to jealousy, because, despite the fact that Jewish people have always been thinly populated in various countries, they have always had a disproportionate number of outstanding public figures.

BUCKY: Since this seems to be such a long-term problem throughout history, do you think that it will ever cease?

EINSTEIN: Perhaps, but only through persistence. Everyone, Jews

and gentiles, must be reasonable and intelligent about it. I
think that Jewish students should have their own student
societies. They should always be courteous, while always
remaining consistent in their views, and not antagonize the
gentiles. One way that it won't be solved is for Jewish people
to take on Christian fashions and manners. They must live
according to their own likes and customs. In this way, it is
entirely possible to be a civilized person, a good citizen, and at
the same time be a faithful Jew who loves his race and honors
his fathers. If these guides are followed, I think that it would
go a long way to considerably reducing anti-Semitism throughout the world.

BUCKY: I recall one time when you were invited by the French
government to take part in a manifestation against anti-Semitism. At that time, you refused to participate. Why was that?

EINSTEIN: This was a somewhat technical problem. At that time, I
was still a German citizen, although I did not reside in Germany. I had perceived the intent of this demonstration as being
aimed at the German government, rather than at anti-Semitism
as a principle. Therefore, strictly as a technical matter, my
participation could have been judged as treasonous. In addition to that, I felt that the effectiveness of such a campaign
would be increased if non-Jewish people were in the forefront,
rather than obvious Jewish people such as myself.

BUCKY: Do you think that there is any such thing as a "Jewish
point of view?"

EINSTEIN: No, definitely not. I will qualify this only by saying that
perhaps only philosophically is there a Jewish point of view. I
do not even see Judaism as a creed. I think that the so-called
Judaic God is really just a negation of superstition.

BUCKY: There seems to be one major contradiction in your overall
philosophy, Professor, and that stems from your open support
of Zionism. In most of your other statements and in your
informal conversations with me, you have always held that
nationalism is one of the roots of evil in the modern world.
And yet, you very strongly support the rights of the Jews to a
national homeland. How do you justify this?

EINSTEIN: I think that it is justified in this special case because the world has forced the Jews to entrench themselves with the continued existence of anti-Semitism.

BUCKY: But you are aware, of course, of some of the practical problems that Israel faces. I myself have never been able to accept Israel as an ideal solution for the Jews for several reasons. First, Israel's right to Palestine's land raises many major moral and legal questions. Second, I think that England just washed their hands of responsibility in this area. Third, I don't think that the Jews could thoroughly realize all of their hopes and dreams in Israel, because it is so geographically limited. And fourth, I see nothing but strife between the Jews and the surrounding Arab countries.

EINSTEIN: The problem is difficult, but not insurmountable. I think that it could probably be solved in the following way. I believe that a group or council should be formed, equally represented by Jews and Arabs with no political leanings or affiliations. Each side should be represented by an attorney, a person from a medical background, and a representative of the people, perhaps a workingman selected by each country's trade unions. One other person in each group should be familiar with efficient organization so that the groups can work together effectively. These two groups should meet regularly to discuss mutual problems and they should hold their meetings secretly and not even discuss them privately once outside of the meetings.

BUCKY: How would they ever achieve this level of secrecy? Human beings find this difficult, especially in family surroundings.

EINSTEIN: Well, it would not be total secrecy. If a decision was reached in which at least three of the members of each side agreed, then this decision could be publicized—not as individuals but as a decision of the council itself. But some secrecy would be required so that the members would not be biased by outside pressure.

BUCKY: This idea sounds very similar to the United Nations.

EINSTEIN: Yes, it is, actually, especially as it would have no definite powers. It would only have the function of smoothing out problems between Israel and the Arabic states.

CHAPTER SIX

Einstein and Education

1. Einstein the Teacher

Einstein was as gentle as a teacher as he was as a man in general. As will be seen from the conversation that follows, he had an intense aversion to undue force in the classroom as well as to restrictions on exploration and natural curiosity. These negative qualities, he felt, worked toward destroying the natural joy that most students will bring to their studies if they were only allowed to find their own level of interest in school.

He once gave me an example that was illustrative of this attitude. He said that even if one were to take a wild animal, whose natural proclivity is to eat raw meat, and continually beat the animal when he was hungry and attempted to eat the raw meat, one could eventually discourage that animal from following his natural bent.

So Einstein developed a very personal philosophy of teaching. He felt that the weakness of most teachers was that they did not attempt to put themselves in their students' places and try to think as they might. They were like parents who expect their children to act, think, and react like adults. Einstein believed that the good teacher must place himself inside the minds of his students.

To understand what sort of teacher Einstein was in those few brief episodes in which he actually taught, it might be educational to consider the teacher who most influenced him in his own school days, for in the academic world, teachers often model themselves after their idols.

In this respect, a Professor Muehlberg seems to fit the bill. He taught chemistry and the natural sciences at the Kantonschule of Aarau. Einstein was touched by his philosophy of education, which was that spiritual ability, will, and zest for discovering new things were more important than the gaining of momentary, fleeting knowledge.

He was also impressed by Professor Muehlberg because, as conservator of the Museum of Natural History, the professor was always taking his students outdoors to demonstrate the wonders of nature. Einstein told me how, on one of these jaunts, the professor asked him, "Albert, do you think that the different layers of rock on the mountain go from the bottom to the top or from the top to the bottom?" Einstein said his reply was, "Professor, to me it does not make any difference one way or the other."

Einstein's first thoughts about becoming a teacher came when he was about sixteen years old. At that time, he said, his parents' business had failed and money was running out, jeopardizing the furtherance of his studies. Frantic, his parents urged him to take up something practical and, perhaps, even to contribute toward helping the family financially.

As a result, Einstein began to think seriously of becoming a teacher, but a very special teacher, of the sort that he would have liked being taught by. In the end, he put these thoughts aside, opting instead for the education that would eventually lead him on to greater glories. But he often told me that he would have been very happy teaching in his own style, making children happy, and guiding them in a way that he felt had been lacking in his own case.

Einstein actually never had an opportunity to teach until he was twenty-nine years old. As Ronald Clark wrote in his biography, *Einstein: The Life and Times,* "The Einstein of the early 1900's was not only a scientist of minor academic qualifications who had launched an obscure theory on the world. He was also the man who failed to fit in or to conform, the disrespector of professors . . . who although approaching the age of thirty still seemed to prefer the company of students."

His first application to lecture at the University of Bern was rejected. But one year later, at the behest of the physicist Alfred Kleiner, the university's decision was reversed. So, at twenty-nine, he settled in to teaching "The Theory of Radiation" to only four students. This was whittled down to one student in the next term, so that Einstein, happily, was able to abandon formality and adjourn the class to his own rooms. So it was that his first venture into teaching was not a very lustrous one.

Two years later, Einstein was appointed a full professor at the University of Prague. But this appointment was only to last eighteen months. Einstein was disenchanted with having to lecture at set times on set days. So he was soon looking to return to Switzerland.

The next year (after turning down a lecture series at Columbia University in New York), Einstein began an appointment that was supposed to last for ten years at the Swiss Federal Polytechnic School (known as ETH). His method here was to hold weekly afternoon colloquia to discuss new work. Unlike his intimate classes at the university, these classes were jammed with students and other professors. As classes ended, Einstein would often invite students to follow him to the cafe to continue their discussions.

From that time on, Einstein's connections with teaching were restricted to formal lecture series at various universities around the world. As a result of his winning the Nobel Prize in 1919, his name was in constant demand for such lecture assignments.

There was another facet of Einstein's teaching, and that was the hundreds of physics and mathematics students who wrote to him from all over the world seeking answers to perplexing questions. I'll never know how Einstein found time to personally answer all of his mail, but somehow he did just that. In that respect, he was also serving an important teacher's role. But, even then, he always found a way to do it that would not stifle the curiosity or the problem-solving facility of his questioner.

On one such occasion, Einstein wrote the following letter to my father:

> I have just received a very interesting mathematical problem sent to me in a letter from a young scientist. He deduces a mathematical proposition which is undoubtedly correct and original. He endeavors to prove the correctness of his presumption mathematically. Unfortunately, there are two faulty arrangements in his calculation. In spite of them, he evinced the correct result. He conceived the proposition emotionally but failed in its mathematical proof. I have corrected the

calculations but in order not to compcte with the young man as to the priority of the correct calculation and so create a feeling of dependency in him, I wrote him that the proposition is true but that my correction of his faulty calculation would be at his disposal at any time that he would like to have it. In such a way, he retains the unrestricted priority of the idea and can find the correct solution himself without becoming dependent on me.

Even his final position, at the Institute for Advanced Studies, while in a strictly academic setting, did not involve him in actual teaching but rather in his own research.

Einstein had confided in me during the conversation that follows that his biggest regret in life was that he didn't get to teach young children. This is, indeed, unfortunate, for Einstein had such a joyful love of his subject that he could easily have transferred it to younger children. And he had an ability to simplify technical difficulties that would have been an asset in teaching the young.

Two incidents brought home this special knack of simplification to me. The first was one time when we had a discussion concerning the speed of light, which he told me was always the same, no matter what the speed may be of the object that produces the light. I had the hardest time understanding this concept, until he explained it this way: "When you are riding in a rowboat at a certain speed and you take a rudder and stir it in the water, creating waves, these waves will travel at the same speed whether the boat is standing still or moving forward."

The second incident occurred one day when I was walking with him at Watch Hill, Rhode Island. I had always been perplexed as to why, when you stand on dry sand at the beach, the weight of your body makes your feet sink into the sand until you reach a certain depth, while, on the other hand, if you walk near the water line where the sand is moist, the surface will fully support your body. When I put the question to Einstein, he smiled and explained the cause in one easy sentence: "The surface tension created by the small water particles between each grain of

sand is the secret of holding them together with strength suffi-
cient to support the weight of the average human body."

Considering this innate ability to explain complex theories so
simply, it is, indeed, a shame that more students weren't able to
benefit from his direct teaching. But that was the balance that the
world had to accept in order that Einstein could have the freedom
and time to develop his theories.

2. Conversation: On Education

BUCKY: Professor Einstein, what do you feel to be the most important role of education in the modern world?

EINSTEIN: Man, I feel, is most properly evaluated in relation to
what he gives rather than what he receives. Therefore, people
must be trained into this attitude of giving to their fellow man.
If humanity is to benefit from each of its members, people
must be trained from youth and, at the same time, school
should be a pleasurable experience so that those being educated do not, in rebelling against the school, also rebel against
the humanistic philosophy that the school might be trying to
inculcate.

Only then, later in life, will the people readily do useful
things for their communities as a whole. I think that this is the
primary work of a good school. It is unfortunate that so many
pupils dislike the idea of even going to school. But often it is
the schools' fault because they exert an undue amount of force
and pressure on students.

BUCKY: What exactly do you mean by undue force and pressure?

EINSTEIN: Well, just the fact of examinations alone is enough. I
remember when I was in school and examinations would be
scheduled, I would feel under such strain that I felt, rather than
going to take a test, that instead, I was walking to the guillo-
tine. I'm surprised, actually, that the desire for education among
today's youth isn't even more restrained than it is.

BUCKY: What else do you consider to be too much pressure for
students?

EINSTEIN: Let me think. Well, yes, I think that it is absolutely

ridiculous for children to be forced to memorize historical
dates. If there ever should be a need for these dates, any
person who has any interest in history certainly would be
capable of looking up these dates in history books.

BUCKY: But perhaps teachers only insist upon this to train and
develop the memory.

EINSTEIN: If that is the case, then they should use material which
is of more use to him practically in life instead of obsolete
history dates. But this is all just part of the greater problem of
improper methods of teaching. Teachers, for the most part, just
don't know how to teach. They forget that their students are
not as naturally excited about the subjects as are the teachers.
A qualified teacher should have the ability or gift of presenting
his subject to his students in such a way as to make it interesting and meaningful to them.

I'll give you an example. When I was a little boy, I remember asking my Uncle Albert to explain to me what algebra is.
Uncle Albert explained it this way: "Well, I will tell you; we
are going hunting for a little animal and we do not know its
name. For that reason, we call it 'X.' When we get our game,
we take it prisoner and only then do we determine what its
name should be." That little tale brought the mysteries of algebra down to a personal level.

BUCKY: Do you feel that the problem with teaching methods that
you mentioned before is a problem only of our time or do you
think that it has always been a problem?

EINSTEIN: Oh, yes, it has always been with us. In fact, I formed my
judgments of what constitutes good teaching methods by experiencing bad methods in action in my own schooling. From
those experiences, I learned that freer teaching forms as well
as giving students a freer selection of subjects that they can
utilize also makes both the teachers and students realize more
strikingly the importance of their respective jobs and makes
the whole educational experience a happier one. Without
this kind of educational freedom, the student's mind will only
rot, for human beings are not machines and can't be treated
like machines.

BUCKY: Do you think that teachers can learn to be freer in their methods, or are they trapped by the system or by their own limitations?

EINSTEIN: In order to create a good teacher, the seed must first be there. What I mean by this is that the most important function of a good teacher is that he have the proper psychological make-up. In this way, he can understand his pupils' needs. Even if such a teacher lacks all of the required knowledge, he can always obtain that knowledge from books or from experience. But the most knowledgeable teacher in the world who does not understand the psychology of dealing with his pupils will make a bad teacher.

BUCKY: Do you think that the systems of teaching are any better at the university level—either when you attended or today?

EINSTEIN: It depends where you are. In most American universities, for instance, attendance at lectures is compulsory. I can't imagine how I could ever have studied in an American college for that reason alone. In Europe, there is much more freedom of attendance, which frees the student to dig more deeply into his subject on his own. Those who are interested in the subject will take advantage of the extra time to learn more. Those who abuse the privilege—well, what does it matter? They won't pursue the subject, anyway.

BUCKY: Are there any other differences that you think are significant?

EINSTEIN: Well, there are differences in the matter of examinations—that curse of education. Students are forced to learn so many unnecessary things, in the name of examinations. As far as I was concerned, after examinations my mind was handicapped for quite some time for scientific exploration and analysis. My mental capacity was exhausted by having had to memorize useless information. But, although all countries basically have examinations as part of their systems, not all have it to the same degree. For example, in Switzerland, where I attended university, there were only two major examinations. But there were many more in the German colleges.

BUCKY: Do you think, then, that the American system of universities is inferior?

EINSTEIN: The European system is better in the sense that I mentioned before. That is, the average European college is not interested in whether a student attends classes, provided that that they pass their exams satisfactorily at the proper time. In the United States, by comparison, because of compulsory attendance, the average American student actually studies a much greater volume of information. Because of all this cramming that is required, the American student does not become as adept at logical thinking.

BUCKY: So what country, then, do you feel has the best system of education?

EINSTEIN: I think that the English school system comes nearest to the perfect one. Those countries that come nearest to force, fear, authority, or harsh treatment have the worst systems. In that respect, I think that Germany and Russia use those principles more than do other countries, whereas schools in the United States and Switzerland and, as I said, England, are much better in that respect.

BUCKY: But, Professor, the English system has always had a reputation for strictness. This would seem to be a contradiction.

EINSTEIN: I understand why you might think this, for it doesn't seem to be consistent with my opinions about freedom. Let me put it this way: I don't mean to imply that strictness is in itself wrong, provided that it is within its limitations and does not restrict individual thinking. By freedom in education, I only mean that somebody should not be made or forced to learn anything for which he is not naturally inclined. But, of course, within that framework, strictness and rules are a necessary thing.

BUCKY: What is your opinion about the more specialized training that seems to prevail nowadays in schools all over the world?

EINSTEIN: I do not believe that the development of specialties is nearly as important in schooling as the ability for independent thinking and judgment. But in this respect, I may be fighting a losing battle because specialization seems to be an irreversible trend. It almost goes hand-in-hand with the mania for efficiency. Unfortunately, I think that efficiency, as such, is more desired in our time by most people than are right values or selecting the proper materials to teach from.

BUCKY: What do you believe is the most important aspect of education?

EINSTEIN: Probably the most valuable asset in education is reading. The teaching that one receives is all well and good, but the teaching is always to some extent inseparable from the personality of the teacher. If the teacher has a bad personality, the students will often reject a subject that might normally be of interest to them. However, when one is interested in a subject and reads a book about it, he has a unique opportunity to grasp the essentials of the subject without intermediaries and, thus, without being influenced in any way by other people.

BUCKY: Are you pessimistic about the future of learning?

EINSTEIN: I don't like to be negative, but sometimes I really think that knowledge, taken by itself, is dead. It takes good teachers and schools to make it come alive again.

BUCKY: How do you think that we can accomplish this?

EINSTEIN: Well, it has to start with the schools themselves. The atmosphere of the school is more important than the individual teachers because it fosters the over-all learning by allowing the proper environment for it. So, first, I think that a school should be just like a big family or community. I think that the best schools are those in which most of the teachers were at one time students there themselves because in that way a greater bond is forged. There should be also as much freedom for the teachers as for the students in selecting what course material they will use. When committees or school boards start meddling in choosing text books and teaching methods, then true learning is buried. In all cases, the pleasure of learning should be fostered and, through it, the recognition of personal accomplishment. And, believe it or not, there are some ideal schools like this, and wherever they exist, I have observed the impossible to happen—that is, the students actually prefer being in school to being on vacation.

BUCKY: How about physical education? Many schools place a great emphasis on sporting activities.

EINSTEIN: I can't really see how a practice of a physical sport helps anyone's general education, except possibly as a means of generating energy to enable the student to concentrate more fully on his studies. That is not to denigrate the physical, because I believe that the greatest and most important phases of a person's education are when he actually physically performs certain functions, for instance when a child first learns to write.

BUCKY: Looking back on all of your life, with all of its connections with universities, do you have any regrets that you didn't do more in the way of actually teaching?

EINSTEIN: Believe it or not, that really is one of my deepest regrets. I regret this because I would have liked to have had more contact with children. There has always been something about the innocence and freshness of young children that appeals to me and brings me great enjoyment to be with them. And they are so open to knowledge. I have never really found it difficult to explain basic laws of nature to children. When you reach them at their level, you can read in their eyes their genuine interest and appreciation.

Actually, I have always been amazed at the questions that children ask about science. For the most part, they are much more logical than many questions that have been asked of me by adults, even by professional people. And also, they are not afraid to ask questions. Adults are too inhibited and afraid to ask "stupid" questions. But in my vocabulary, the word "stupid" does not exist as far as mathematics and the sciences are concerned. This is where many teachers go wrong. They blame their inability to get through to somebody on that person's being stupid, instead of on their own lack of patience or unwillingness to change their own teaching approach.

I'll give you an example. There are many persons who consider themselves to be "stupid" in regard to science and mathematics. Yet, these same people make excellent automobile drivers and, in many cases, can tear an automobile up inside and out and put it back together again. Why? Because they are supremely interested in that car. Well, it is the teacher's duty to find what facet of his subject or what approach will strike each individual student as interesting. And that is a great challenge. Anybody can teach someone who adapts quickly to learning, but it takes a real teacher to reach those pupils who are mentally slower.

CHAPTER SEVEN

Einstein and His Family

1. A Private Look

Tolstoi, in his great novel, *Anna Karenina,* wrote: "All happy families resemble one another; every unhappy family is unhappy in its own fashion." This quotation comes to me when I think back over Einstein and his family, for he and they had a mix of both happiness and unhappiness.

Since I was fortunate to have known Einstein for over twenty years, I had the opportunity to become acquainted, as well, with most of the members of his family who mattered to him, except his father, his mother, and his first wife. Since the friendship between the Einsteins and my family allowed me to observe the great scientist and his family in unguarded leisure, I had a unique perspective. In fact, these private glimpses were afforded me to an extent perhaps unsurpassed by any other living person besides Einstein's stepdaughter Margot, who lived in the simple frame house on Mercer Street in Princeton until her own death, over three decades after Einstein's.

As far as Einstein's early life is concerned, the facts are well-recorded. He was born on 14 March 1879 at 135 Bahnhofstrasse in Ulm, Germany. Most of his family were small tradesmen. Einstein probably got his penchant for mathematical problems from his father who was gifted in this area, but unfortunately could not attend college because of his own family's financial plight. Einstein also probably got his taste for music along with his interest in the violin from his mother, the former Pauline Koch.

His father owned an electrical supply shop in Ulm during Einstein's first year, but his brother—Einstein's uncle Jacob—induced him to move his store to Munich in 1880. There, the elder Einstein became involved in making arc lights, dynamos, and measuring instruments, but the business failed, leaving the family in a poor financial condition. Under the circumstances, Einstein was fortunate that he was not forced to follow in his father's footsteps and forgo higher education.

His first marriage was a misfortune—and out of it came misfortune aplenty. There is a certain difficulty that all great minds experience in trying to assimilate themselves into the formal bonds that ordinary men subject themselves to. "He that hath wife and children," Francis Bacon wrote, "hath given hostages to fortune; for they are impediments to great enterprises, either of virtue or of mischief."

Einstein once told me that he married Mileva Maric because he felt sorry for her. Mileva, he said, was unlikeable, she was ugly, she limped, and, generally, no one wanted anything to do with her. When his circle of friends discovered Einstein's intention to marry her, they all tried to talk him out of it.

Ultimately, the pressures of his great work were felt in the extreme by Mileva and by both of the sons who issued from their union—Eduard and Hans Albert. Eduard was humble and brilliant and perhaps felt the pressure the most, for at a young age he was diagnosed as a schizophrenic and was institutionalized. Herta, the Einsteins' maid in Berlin and Caputh, once told me how, whenever Eduard would be allowed out to visit, he would sit at the family's grand piano and pound the keyboard up and down the scales in the manner of a madman.

In the very year that Einstein was awarded the Nobel Prize, he and Mileva were divorced. One of the pressures on his marriage was his constant moving from Switzerland to Czechoslovakia and back. Mileva found this hard to bear, especially as she had started out, herself, in Serbia. But perhaps even more important in destroying the marriage was Mileva's jealousy over Einstein's notoriety and his work. She also was a physicist but one obviously not in her husband's league.

Recently, some scholars have cited letters from Einstein to Mileva early in their marriage in which he refers to the great theories upon which he was working as "our work." Upon such flimsy evidence do these scholars attempt to construct a new picture of Einstein (conveniently in keeping with the modern penchant for disparaging men's work in favor of women's) as only an equal partner in scientific collaboration with his first wife.

Anyone with any wisdom can sense in these letters a young husband's beneficent indulgence of his wife in his references to "our work." In fact, as Jeremy Bernstein points out in his 6 July 1987 *New Yorker* article, "Einstein When Young," in Einstein's 1905 paper on the "Electrodynamics of Moving Bodies," he thanks for "loyal assistance" only his "friend and colleague," the engineer Michele Besso, to whom he is "indebted . . . for several valuable suggestions." Dr. John Stachel, editor of the Einstein papers, has expressed the opinion that Mileva was probably a "sounding board" rather than a contributor to Einstein's ideas. In fact, Einstein often said that it was impossible for him to discuss his work with her.

In the end, he came to detest his first wife, and these feelings influenced him long after their divorce. He clung to what today would be socially taboo opinions about women and physics. He once told one of his female students that women are not gifted as theoretical physicists and that he would never allow a daughter of his to study physics. But perhaps we can be charitable and say that these opinions were colored by his unfortunate first marriage.

That catastrophic marriage, though, did not prevent him from entering into a second one—"the triumph of hope over experience," as Samuel Johnson had labeled a friend's second marriage. This time, he married a distant cousin, Elsa Einstein, a more homely girl, who brought with her two daughters, Margot and Ilse, from a previous marriage. Here was a girl more to Einstein's liking. As he once put it, "I'm glad that my second wife doesn't know anything about science."

Actually, in today's terms, Einstein would have been considered a classic male chauvinist. He once wrote in a letter to a friend, a Dr. Muesham in Haifa, that his definition of a good wife was someone who stood somewhere between a pig and a chronic cleaner. It would seem that Mileva may have fit the first bill, while Elsa fit the latter.

But Elsa did know a lot about organizing Einstein, and that, in its way, brought its own tensions. Elsa accused Einstein of being a male chauvinist and complained that she waited on him hand and foot and received no sympathy or tenderness in return. On the other hand, she was fiercely supportive of his struggles to unravel the secrets of the universe.

Elsa was a gentle and kind woman and I often suspected that she got a bigger kick out of Einstein's fame and publicity than did Einstein himself. In fact, one of their recurring arguments was over the fact that she kept Einstein circulating publicly by accepting many more social invitations than he would have liked (what he would have liked was zero invitations, for he truly disliked such occasions).

I also remember Elsa as a good and sincere person, one who was extremely considerate of others. Many times she would try to explain to Einstein the viewpoints of others when he didn't understand them as quickly as did she. She was quite nearsighted, but a strain of vanity inhibited her from wearing eyeglasses, which made for some amusing incidents, such as when she would try to find her keys or cut Albert's hair.

On one social occasion, this condition resulted in some embarrassment to Elsa and great amusement to observers. It was at a dinner given at the Waldorf-Astoria Hotel in New York. I was fortunate to be seated next to Einstein's wife during dinner. The settings were gracious in the style that one would expect from the great hotel, and on the table in front of Elsa rested a bouquet of flowers. Elsa, perhaps extremely hungry or perhaps just impatient, saw something quite different in her near-sightedness, and took her knife and fork to the flowers, thinking them to be her salad.

Often, she wouldn't recognize people she knew, and she was constantly bumping into objects. And because of this severe nearsightedness she tended to be very nervous.

She kept a pleasant and orderly house for Einstein while managing also to coordinate all of his functions. At the same time, she had to protect him from his own naiveté. In Germany, she used to say she was afraid some salesman would talk Einstein into buying an elevator for their one-story house in Caputh!

Elsa also had to look after Einstein's dress, since he was totally oblivious to matters of this sort. I distinctly remember one time when she came home with six new shirts, all of which had very attractive cuffs. When he saw them, Einstein scowled and said, "I really don't like these new shirts." He complained that the sleeves were too long and baggy, and he ordered his maid, who was also a seamstress, to simply cut off the cuffs.

Elsa also kept a very tight rein over their finances. Most of us who knew them thought she went a bit overboard in her thriftiness, considering the amount of money that they had and their relatively inexpensive lifestyle. This tightness, though, was another source of violent arguments between them, as Einstein felt that he never had enough money in his pockets.

In all, I think Einstein realized that men such as he, who attempt to unravel the mysteries of the universe or who are deeply involved in any of the arts, have great difficulties in adjusting to married life. In one unguarded moment, he confessed to me that each personal tie was a form of torture for him, that each bond was often intolerable. As he put it, "every handcuff bothers me." When he said this, I asked him, "Suppose that you had an intelligent wife who would stay in the background and have an understanding for everything that you feel and who would leave you alone and would not restrict you or put limitations on you in any way. Would you then have been happy?" Einstein smiled broadly at my utopian suggestion and said, "Of course I would!"

Probably the one person who was closest to him throughout his long life was his sister, Maja, who outlasted Einstein's childhood, both of his marriages, and even his second son and one of his step-daughters. In fact, the only relative who lived beyond Maja was Einstein's older step-daughter, Margot. (Maja's existence might have come as a shock to one of the United States' more famous newspapers, the *New York Daily News,* which once included a photo of Einstein among a group of famous people who were "only children.")

Maja was a wonderful person—a great human being as well as a very educated one. From her, Einstein developed his great love of Italian food. She was an expert in cooking Italian dishes and taught his German maid, Herta, how to prepare them.

When he was next to his sister, one could imagine they were twins, so similar in appearance were they, and they had exactly the same philosophy of life. Thus when Maja came to Princeton and moved in with the Einsteins Albert was thrilled. She also added a musical dimension to the house, as she was a fine pianist. Often, the house on Mercer Street resounded to the sound of Maja's grand piano and the accompaniment of Albert's fiddling.

Maja was also a strict vegetarian, not so much for health reasons as for the fact that she loved animals so much that she could not bear to eat them. It is peculiar, though, that the one exception to this rule was that she loved hotdogs. Einstein used to joke about this, saying, "Well, it is very simply answered. Maja eats hotdogs because she regards the hotdog as a vegetable."

Maja died three and a half years before her famous brother, and that was indeed a sad passing for him to bear. Toward the end, she spent most of her time in bed in the Princeton home, and he would come every night to sit on her bed. There he would read her famous works of history, which she enjoyed, as well as the latest news and other items of interest to her.

Einstein also liked his step-daughters, Ilse and Margot. But Ilse died a very painful death in Paris in 1934—a death that her mother, Elsa, never really got over. Ilse had been married to Dr. Rudolf Kayser, a plain, simple, and modest man who was an editor with the S. Fischer Publishing House in Germany.

Quite the opposite was Margot's husband, Dmitri Marianoff, a Russian who was involved in the Soviet movie industry. Marianoff, a man with deceitful habits that caused many people to dislike him, was also untrue to Margot, as she discovered when she found bills from Paris for flowers that he had sent to lady friends.

Margot divorced him after seven years of marriage. Later, when he moved to the United States, he became involved in some un-ethical activities involving the U.S. Department of Agriculture. He died of a malignancy in the 1930s.

Both Kayser and Marianoff wrote books about Einstein, detailing their experiences in the family, but he rejected Marianoff's work, contending that much of it was untrue.

Margot stayed close to Einstein throughout his life and remained in his Princeton home until her death. When she moved into the Princeton home, Margot immediately became one of his closest confidants. Often, Einstein would have problems in his laboratory and he would come alone for lunch. There, after looking glum and pale and saying hardly a word during lunch, he would turn to Margot and say, "Margot, would you like to take a little walk—it would do us both good." Their walks would, indeed, be therapeutic for Einstein, and he would return to his work with renewed vigor.

Margot was also a talented person in her own right, an extraordinarily sensitive artist whose favored medium was sculpture. When she joined the household in the mid-1930s, she brought with her about a dozen relatively small pieces of her own work, in terra cotta, bronze, clay, wood, and wax. I recall how, on our family's visits to the Einsteins, pieces such as a little organ-grinder done in tissue paper, wax, and bits of metal would be scattered throughout the house.

Her pieces ran the gamut from busts in clay to seated women (with exceptionally crafted and detailed faces and hands), dolls, and wooden ducks. One was a seated Russian peasant woman in a railway station, carved in oak, an extremely difficult medium for wood-carving.

Margot was physically very sensitive and fragile and reacted strongly to changes in atmospheric pressure and humidity. For that reason, she preferred the mountains to the sea. Her love for animals was reflected in her affection for my dog, Chico, a wire-hair, who became one of her favorite pets. (Chico was actually quite a privileged dog—he once had the honor of being mentioned in the well-known "Profiles" column of *The New Yorker* magazine, and when he died, at the age of fifteen, his body was buried in Einstein's back garden!).

Despite the fact that Margot was never fully comfortable in Princeton (she always expressed the desire to escape the cloisteral stolidity of Princeton to wander through the streets of New York's vibrant East Side), she ended up staying in Princeton for over a half-century. In those years, she acquired an increasingly alarmed social consciousness, decrying the fact that modern Western society seemed to have lost the ability to nurture its artists—the people she liked to call "our culture-bearers."

(I have included at the end of this chapter a Part Three, which is the last interview, so to speak, that Einstein's step-daughter ever gave, recorded in 1986, only shortly before Margot's death, during a private luncheon at the Mercer Street house.)

Probably the real sadness of Einstein's life involved his relationship with his eldest son, Hans Albert. I met Hans for the first time in 1937 and thereafter had the opportunity to get to know him very well. I once took him around the United States by automobile for three months, a trip that covered over 10,000 miles. During this trip, we visited major universities all over the country, as Hans was looking into getting placement as a professor of hydraulic engineering.

Hans Albert Einstein also had another purpose during this trip, which was to inspect American hydraulic works, such as the Hoover Dam, as the tremendous size and extent of America's engineering imagination had attracted much attention in Europe. (At the time, Hans was living in Switzerland, where the government was experiencing problems with flood control.)

Our extensive tour took us to such stop-overs as Salt Lake City, Los Angeles, Iowa City, Knoxville (where a picture caption in that city's newspaper erroneously identified me as the son of Albert Einstein), Vicksburg, Cleveland, Chicago, Detroit, and Indianapolis. Such magic did the Einstein name have, as it still does, that wherever we went, even though Hans was only the son of the great scientist, we ended up on the front pages of the local newspapers.

In 1938, the year following our trip, Hans Albert migrated to the United States, partly motivated by his preoccupation with large rivers in flat terrain, where sedimentation becomes a problem (in Switzerland, he had dealt for the most part only with mountain streams).

Immediately upon his emigration to America, Hans became a research engineer with the Agricultural Experiment Station in Clemson, South Carolina. Following this, he worked until 1947 as a research engineer with the United States Department of Agriculture at the California Institute of Technology in Pasadena. Then, in 1947, he became an associate professor at the University of California in Berkeley, later becoming a full professor of civil engineering.

Hans Albert was truly a chip off the old block. He hated publicity, and during our extended trip I was also charged with using many subterfuges so that the younger Einstein's privacy could be assured. Also Hans, like his father, was obsessed with truthful-

107

ness, and if any friend should ever be caught in a lie, it would become impossible for Hans ever again to proffer his friendship.

Even in physical appearance, Hans was very much a mirror of his father. His hair was bushy like his father's, and his manner of speaking also bore a tremendous resemblance to that of the elder Einstein.

Hans also had his father's aversion to luxuries as evidenced by the fact that, when he first came to America, he built a simple home in Greensboro, North Carolina, with his own hands.

But while there were many similarities between Hans and the great physicist, there were also many problems between them. It can be said without stretching matters that the two had a love-hate relationship with, perhaps, "hate" coming out a little on top. Hans was always embarrassed by his father's dress, with the result that Hans's only concession to luxury was to dress in a dapper fashion.

Many of Hans's troubles with his father stemmed from the fact that Hans was very impressionable and, as a result, was often swayed by philosophies forced upon him by his two wives, one after the other. Thus, during his first marriage, to Freida Knecht, who held a doctoral degree in German language and literature and taught at the University of Zurich, Hans became a Christian Scientist. As a result of the antimedical beliefs of this religion, his wife lost a child. Because of this, although Hans fairly worshipped his father, the elder Einstein gave Hans hell for converting from Judaism—even though Albert himself did not formally follow his faith. Freida died suddenly in 1958, and in 1959 Hans remarried, this time to Elizabeth Roboz, also a Ph.D., who was a clinical professor of neurology at the University of California, San Francisco, Medical Center.

Hans's second wife was a leftist who became embroiled in political problems with the United States government. True to his character, Hans adopted his wife's radical beliefs.

Because of the religious friction between Albert and Hans, Einstein practically cut his son out of his will, leaving half of his estate to Helen Dukas and half to his step-daughter Margot. (Perhaps this was fuel for Hans's belief that his father and Miss Dukas had been lovers, of which more in the following chapter.)

The entire episode was sad for all concerned. Dukas and Mar-

Vacationing together in Watch Hill, Rhode Island, in 1934.
From left: Gustav, Frieda, and Peter A. Bucky, Elsa and Albert
Einstein, and a friend.

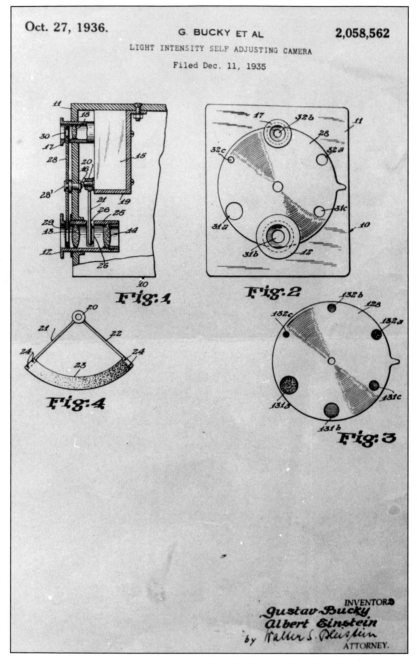

Drawing for patent on camera that Dr. Gustav Bucky and
Einstein invented.

Photograph autographed by "A. Einstein" to "Peter Bucky
with Sincere Wishes."

UNITED STATES PATENT OFFICE

2,058,562

LIGHT INTENSITY SELF-ADJUSTING CAMERA

Gustav Bucky, New York, N. Y., and Albert Einstein, Princeton, N. J.

Application December 11, 1935, Serial No. 53,884

9 Claims. (Cl. 95—10)

This invention relates to a camera with a device for automatically adjusting the light intensity, and an object of the invention is to provide means for automatically adapting the light impinging the photographic plate or film of the camera to the light intensity of the surroundings and particularly of the object to be photographed.

A further object of the invention is to provide means for an automatic adjustment of the light intensity without necessitating the use of a power source which may be due to get exhausted after a certain length of time, like an electric battery.

The invention consists in the combination of a camera with a photo-electric cell and a screen of varying penetrability to light, said screen being movable in the path of the light rays passing the camera objective.

Further objects, features and details will be apparent from the following description and the accompanying drawing illustrating an embodiment of the invention. In the drawing are:

Fig. 1 a side elevation of a portion of a camera, as per the invention, partly in section,

Fig. 2 a front elevation of the camera,

Fig. 3 a front elevation of a modified part,

Fig. 4 an elevation of the screen.

Referring now to the figures, 10 is a camera having a front wall 11, which carries the photographic objective 12 with lenses 13 and 14. In the interior of the camera 10, a photo-electric cell forming a unit 15 together with a mechanism for turning a shaft is mounted and secured to the camera by suitable means, as for instance by means of a bracket 16. Such photo-electric cell with the mentioned mechanism for turning a shaft, which may be for instance a mechanism as conventional in a millivoltmeter, is a well-known unit available on the market and is used in exposure meters where the shaft carries a pointer for indicating the correct length of exposure, as for instance the "Weston Photronic photo-electric cell". This photo-electric cell unit 15 per se does not form part of the present invention and is therefore shown merely in its outlines. 16 is the shaft adapted to be actuated by said photo-electric cell unit. The unit 15 receives light through a tubular fixture 17 in front wall 11 with or without the help of a lens 18 in the aperture of fixture 17. With shaft 16, a member 20 is rigidly connected, which comprises two radial arms 21 and 22. A screen 23 having the shape of a ring segment is stretched between the ends of arms 21 and 22 and secured to these arms for instance by means of rivets 24. Screen 23 is made of a transparent, preferably of a celluloid-like material. The transparency of the screen is decreased from one end to the other, from its maximum to a minimum. This is done by shading it from clear over gray to black as indicated in Fig. 4. This screen is so arranged that it may swing in the path of the light rays passing through objective 12, and it is furthermore so arranged that the screen portion with maximum transparency is in the path of the rays when the photo-electric cell is not or only very little energized, that means when the light intensity is weakest. The plane in which the screen intersects these light rays is immaterial. We, however, prefer to position the screen between the lenses 13 and 14 for which purpose the objective tube 25 is slitted at 26, because the coincidence of the rays in the space between the lenses permits the screen to be made very narrow. This is important because the movable parts in connection with unit 15 should be made as light as possible in consideration of the very small power output of a photo-electric cell. It is, however, within the scope of this invention to use another kind of photo-sensitive cells as for instance a selenium cell with a battery.

It will be understood that the camera according to our invention may be equipped with any conventional accessorial parts as for instance a shutter, omitted in the drawing in order to avoid overcrowding of lines.

If now the camera is directed with its objective 12 upon the object to be photographed, the aperture or light entrance tube 17 of the photo-electric unit is directed likewise. The light intensity striking the photo-electric unit creates a power which turns the shaft 16 through an angle which is a function of the light intensity. Consequently, the screen 23, is swung between lenses 13 and 14 in such a position that the light impinging the photographic plate or film is adjusted in correspondence with the light entering the photo-electric unit. It is obvious that the increment of alteration of the transparency has to be so chosen from the start, that it corresponds with the angles through which the shaft 16 is turned due to the light intensity, and that it also corresponds with the light desired to impinge the photographic plate.

If a camera is equipped with the device as described, no iris for light reduction is required. In many instances, however, it may be desirable to have different diaphragms or a variable diaphragm for the objective in the conventional manner, and to use the automatic adjuster only for taking care of such alterations of the light which occur after the camera has been set for taking a photograph with a definite shutter speed. This may be the case particularly with cinematographic cameras. It also may be desirable to voluntarily alter the aperture of the objective in correspondence with the sensitivity of the emulsion of the film or plate used in each particular case. If, however, the aperture of the objective is variable in a voluntary manner, the self-adjusting device may not always produce proper correction for the alterations of the light. In

Dr. Gustav Bucky, the author's father.

The author's family with the Einsteins in one of the open-air rides that delighted Albert. From left: Maja (Albert's sister) and Frieda Einstein, Thomas (the author's brother) and Gustav Bucky, and Albert.

Gustav Bucky with Einstein on another vacation in Watch Hill, in 1936.

The *Journal American*, informed by the author, reported the news nine hours after Einstein's death.

Maja and Albert Einstein with daughter of Gustav Bucky's accountant; the accountant, Mr. Mattersdorf; and Dr. Bucky.

Einstein the sailor, in photograph inscribed "From the conscientious helmsman to his dear friend Bucky."

A picture of the poem that Einstein wrote to the author in his own handwriting together with the translation of the poem on opposite page.

A picture of the head of Einstein with his personal dedication.

Elegy, to be sung in two parts by Master Peter and his Mommy

Today I am sending you a poem,
It is not by Schiller, you can guess.
It does not soar proudly in the air,
And its fragrance is very down-to-earth.

Virginia is dangerous,
She does it sweetly and also cleverly.
Mother, on the other hand,
Excels in watchfulness.

We do not envy Master Peter,
The way he is handled by these two.
He twists and turns as well as he can,
As a strong man should.

Anyone who has ever been stuck like this
Has respect for such a thing.
He knows how helpless and confused
Menfolk are in such a situation.

Fury does not achieve anything.
In such delicate matters.
One is plucked and tormented,
But courage! Time heals such wounds.

And the moral of the story
(Which one hardly ever discusses)
Is that the upper half plans and thinks,
While the lower half determines our fate.

A.E /illegible/

A picture of Einstein with
Dr. Gustav Bucky in the
sailboat with dedication.

THE INSTITUTE FOR ADVANCED STUDY
SCHOOL OF MATHEMATICS
PRINCETON, NEW JERSEY

TO WHOM IT MAY CONCERN:

I herewith testify that the camera invented
and produced by Dr.Gustav BUCKY, 5 East 7᷍.
Str.New York City, is - in my opinion - of
considerable value especially for medical
practice and for certain technical applications.
I have witnessed with interest the development
of this invention and the hard work to bring it
to its present perfection.
Dr.Bucky's son,Mr.Peter Bucky, participated a
good deal in this work and it would be an out-
spoken disadvantage for the production of the camera
if he would suddenly be taken away.

May 6,1942   *A. Einstein.*

                    Professor Albert Einstein.

May 28,1942

Mr.Peter A.Bucky
5 East 76.Str.
New York City

Dear Peter:

You have asked me to give you a statement
concerning my opinion on the Coreco Camera which your
father has developed and on which you have collaborated.

I believe that the camera has a number of fine
possibilities which not only pertain to civil use but should
also be of great value for the Army and Navy. It's advantages in
the medical field have been proven through practical experience
pertaining to civil as well as to war work. As your camera sim-
plifies medical photographic records and diagnosis it would be
useful for every medical unit.

This camera will photograph accurately the inside of
the a gas engine cylinder which permits the observation of the
inside of the engine for checking purposes without the need of
dismantling the engine.

With this camera the following advantages are obtained:
a) no adjustment necessary for focusing the object
to be photographed.

b) no adjustment necessary in respect to diaphragm or
exposure time.

c) one can easily take cavity pictures due to its special
lightning arrangement.

d) one can take snapshot pictures of great focal depht.

Cordially yours,

A. Einstein

Professor Albert Einstein.

TO WHOM IT MAY CONCERN:

I know Peter A.BUCKY for twelve years quite
intimately. He is a young man of unquestionable
integrity and I take every responsibility for
his political reliability and absolute loyalty
to the United States.
Mr.Peter A.Bucky's technical knowledge and experience
I believe can be of considerable value in the service.
Dr.Gustav Bucky invented the CORECO CAMERA and Peter
A.Bucky,his son, collaborated in the development.
The camera is -in my opinion - of considerable value
especially for medical practice and for certain technical applications. I have witnessed with interest the
development of this invention and the hard work to bring
it to its present perfection.

May 11,1942   A. Einstein.

                                   Professor Albert Einstein.

THE INSTITUTE FOR ADVANCED STUDY
SCHOOL OF MATHEMATICS
PRINCETON, NEW JERSEY

April 13, 1943

Lt. Peter A. Bucky
New York Medical Dept.
Procurement District
52 Broadway
New York City

Dear Peter:

I am grateful that you have the intention
to demonstrate my ideas about an artificial horizon and
an altitude barometer to the proper military authorities,
and I authorize you herewith to do so.

Having explained to you the essential points
you will be able to explain the matter without special
drawings. I am, of course, willing at any time to give any
desired information.

Yours very sincerely,

A. Einstein.

Professor Albert Einstein.

den 13.April 1943

Lieber Peter,

hier der gewünschte offizielle Brief.
Ich möchte bei dieser Gelegenheit auch sagen, dass
mir das junge Mädchen, das Sie mitgebracht haben, einen
besonders guten Eindruck gemacht hat.

Herzlich grüsst Sie

Ihr

A. Einstein.

Dear Peter:

Herewith the requested official letter*. I would like to take this opportunity
to tell you, that the young girl, which you have brought along, made an
esspecially good impression on me.

Heartily greets you,

your

* His letter of April 13, 1943, concerning his artificial horizon.

got, both protective of Albert's sensitivities, took on the same negative feelings towards Hans even after Albert Einstein died. Often, Hans asked to visit the house in Princeton for nostalgic reasons, but Margot, Dukas, and Otto Nathan, Einstein's literary executor, steadfastly refused to grant him permission. I remember my late wife, Tina, telling me once how Hans had described his frustration at their refusals and how he and she had wept. Often, Tina tried to discuss the matter with Margot to try to persuade her to allow Hans to visit the house, but the result was always the same—Margot would clam up.

On other occasions, when Tina would talk to Margot about Hans, Margot would suggest that at one time Hans had done something terribly wrong to his immediate family as well as to his father. It was never clear whether she was referring to the child who died without medical care. Margot also told my wife that Hans always did things on his own and would never inform his father about what he was doing, either in his personal affairs or in his professional life. The only way the family ever learned about Hans's activities, Margot said, was through second-hand sources.

Margot also said there was additional tension between Einstein and his son because the latter's political leanings were too far to the left (which was an irony, since so many commentators accused Einstein of the same leanings).

Hans finally died in Massachusetts in 1971 of a heart attack without ever having had the opportunity to return to Princeton. But even though he had these difficulties with his renowned father, he was never bitter, and he would often say to Tina and me, "You have one father and one mother—you may disagree with them, but you must still love them."

As a result of Einstein's second son's mental tragedy, there remain today only three living blood descendants of Albert Einstein. They are Hans's son, Bernhard Einstein, who is in engineering research, Hans's daughter, Evelyn, who is married to an anthropologist, and Bernhard's son, Thomas, a doctor residing in Connecticut (who inherited Einstein's beloved violin). It remains to be seen if any of them will leave any progeny with a direct bloodline to Einstein, or if, like so many other great men—Mozart and Beethoven, for instance—Einstein will have no descendants remaining in the twenty-first century to carry on his name, if not his work.

2. A Miscellany of Opinions

BUCKY: Professor, you are a man who has always been followed by criticism, praise, and publicity. And yet, you have always seemed to be impervious to these distractions. How has it been possible for you to live your life without being disturbed or disrupted by the judgments of the outside world?

EINSTEIN: Well, I have considered myself to be very fortunate in that I have been able to do mostly only that which my inner self told me to do. It is really embarrassing to me that I do get so much honor and appreciation for what I do because it might create the impression in some people's minds that I'm just doing these things in order to get these honors. This, of course, is definitely not the case. I am also aware that I do receive much criticism from the outside world for what I do and some people actually get angry at me. But this does not really touch me because I feel that these people do not live in the same world as do I.

BUCKY: But for the most part, you are fortunate in being more respected than criticized, I think.

EINSTEIN: Yes, but this is, in some cases, a double-edged sword. I do not feel at ease with the fact that this popularity sometimes leads people to accept my public or private statements as valid just by virtue of my asserting them. This is dangerous for them, for they are impairing their individuality. Blind faith in what I say stops them from exploring in their own minds whether certain things might actually be different from what I express. I am not, after all, infallible.

BUCKY: It is one thing, of course, for people to criticize your theories. But you are also on the receiving end of criticisms of a more practical nature—namely, your dress habits.

EINSTEIN: This is so superficial! How a person chooses to dress is so unimportant. In any event, you can be pretty sure that the outer appearance of a man is probably misleading. What really matters is how a person is dressed inside. One should draw his attention from others not by his outer appearance but rather by his inner qualities.

BUCKY: What inner qualities do you consider to be the most valued?

EINSTEIN: Most importantly, truth. Real inner beauty is expressed best in a man who will never lie and has no thoughts of deceiving anybody. Also, genuine inner beauty is expressed in a person who has no malice towards anyone. Kindness towards other human beings is also of supreme importance.

BUCKY: What, then, do you consider to be the meaning of life?

EINSTEIN: What is the meaning of human life, or for that matter, the life of any creature? To know the answer to that question means to be religious. All that I can say is that anybody who believes that his function in this world is unproductive or unnecessary is the type of person who does not deserve to be in our world. The man who regards his own life and that of his fellow creatures as meaningless is not merely unhappy but hardly fit for life.

BUCKY: Getting back to your style of dress, what do you say to those who accuse you of drawing attention to yourself through your nonconformity?

EINSTEIN: Believe me, this is not the case. You will probably not believe it that even when I was a little boy I was being spanked for not having on my Sunday clothes at the proper time and also because I did not conform to the usual way of saying, "How do you do?" to our guests. My dress and the way I wear my hair stem solely from my desire for simplicity. It is my feeling that the less that I can get along with in daily life, such as automobiles and socks, the freer I am from these drudgeries. If I don't have my hair cut, then I do not feel the need for a barber.

BUCKY: So you do not feel, as most people do, a desire for simple luxuries?

EINSTEIN: It depends on what you call luxuries. Of course, I like a good bed and good food. But what difference does it make what kind of lodging you have as long as the bed you sleep in is not hard and as long as the food that you eat is not stale and is in large enough quantities so that you do not have to go hungry? Luxuries are things which a human being does not need in order to get along, but which are possessed by people who have more means than the average person and which are sometimes even possessed by people who cannot afford them.

BUCKY: Let us go into some deeper areas, such as the arts. For instance, let us take poetry. Who are some of your favorite poets?

EINSTEIN: Heinrich Heine stands out as my favorite poet, although it saddens me that in my later years, I have had so little opportunity to read his works.

BUCKY: How about writers, in general?

EINSTEIN: I think that the most wonderful book that I ever read was *The Brothers Karamazov* by Dostoevsky. I also enjoy the works of George Bernard Shaw. Unfortunately, there are very few people in this world who understand and perceive the weaknesses and peculiarities of their fellow men. And many of those that do are too selfish or lacking in courage to express their views. But George Bernard Shaw was able to comment on the foibles of mankind and he has done so with an exquisite sense of humor.

BUCKY: Do you enjoy reading biographies of other great people? Or do you, like myself, find that these are too often very dry and uninteresting with too many exaggerations of unimportant matters?

EINSTEIN: It is funny that you tell me this. I feel the same way about most biographies. But there are exceptions and those are the ones that I enjoy reading. When I do, I like to envision my life in connection with the life of the person who is written about. Indeed, I would have enjoyed writing some select biographies, whether they were of people involved with the arts, the sciences, or of people dedicated to anything with passion and with truth. Truth! Now there is the point!

BUCKY: Who are your favorite philosophers?

EINSTEIN: I enjoy reading the works of Schopenhauer and Kant and Plato. But my favorite of all is Spinoza. I subscribe fully to a tribute written to Spinoza by Friedrich Schleiermacher many years ago. I can never forget those words: "The infinity was his beginning and his end, the universe his only and everlasting love. In holy innocence and deep humility he beheld himself mirrored in the eternal world and perceived how he was its most amiable mirror. Wherefore he stands there, alone and unequaled, a master of his art but sublime above the profane rabble, a peerless beacon forever."

BUCKY: One cannot, of course, touch upon the world of psychology without bringing up the name of Sigmund Freud, who has had so much influence upon the twentieth century. And yet, many of his theories have stirred up so much controversy. What are your own feelings about Freud and his work?

EINSTEIN: I have read, of course, many of Freud's works, though I must say that I have many doubts about some of his theories. I think, for instance, that Freud placed much too much emphasis on his dream theories. After all, a junk closet does not bring everything forth. For example, I find it interesting how in a dream not always those items that interest us most are dredged up.

BUCKY: What about Freud's emphasis upon sexual experience as a determinant of one's personality?

EINSTEIN: This is another area where I think that Freud was ill-advised. If one does not recall the sexual context, this is interpreted by Freud as repression. If one does recall the sexual context, this is proof of his theories being correct. This is too self-serving a theory for me to accept and does not allow for any disproof to be accepted. Of course, certain events in our younger days made an impression upon us, but not so great that in later years we are still thinking about it. But on the other hand, Freud was very interesting to read and he was also very witty. And I certainly do not mean to be overly critical. Freud's arguments were so pure in their logic and he always sought the truth foremost. His opinions showed a real sense of responsibility. Indeed, I think that through his increasing popularity, Freud could have a powerful influence in straightening out the human mind and could even help to lead toward the abolition of war.

BUCKY: Are there any psychological theorists whom you prefer to Freud?

EINSTEIN: I find, generally, too much to criticize in most of the other theorists' works. Adler, for instance, was lacking as an authority, and I always had the impression on reading Jung that he was not a very sympathetic human being.

BUCKY: So, in general, you don't believe the crux of modern psychology—that life's experiences influence the development of the inner self?

EINSTEIN: Yes, that is correct. This theory stems from the idea that the personality is deep-rooted, which I do not really believe. Many aspects of our personalities that we consider to be deep-rooted are merely habits. A person can be "transplanted" without any damage and his roots will merely become more "tender" afterwards.

BUCKY: Let's shift to something that might be considered akin to psychology—that is, the idea of extra-sensory perception. These so-called "vibrations" that people receive, or the "sixth sense," seem to me to be unexplainable in terms of natural phenomena or physical logic. What do you think about this subject?

EINSTEIN: Well, I think that the idea really is very natural, or else we would all have been created with elephant hides. I think that these vibrations are continually assaulting us all the time. But what really matters is to either receive them or to repel them, depending upon their utility or goodness. Much of this, of course, has to do with the power of concentration. One can train oneself, after all, to compute the most difficult problems with nothing but a pad, a pencil, and one's mind, despite numerous outside intrusions and interruptions, such as noise, music, or conversation. One who can accomplish this is well-prepared to be a receptor of "vibrations" such as those of which you speak.

BUCKY: We have touched upon a lot of the creative arts. But your field, too, is an art in one sense. So while we are talking of great men whom you look up to, perhaps you might tell me which physicist you respect the most.

EINSTEIN: The man I am going to speak to you about meant more to me personally than anybody else that I have ever met. I refer, of course, to [Hendrik A.] Lorentz. He was the only man I ever met whose character traits were so ideal that it was always a pleasure to be in his company. Unfortunately, people who accomplish a great deal in life develop also a great stubbornness and often a feeling of superiority over others. But Lorentz never took on these bad traits. In fact, he would make haste to assert someone else's correctness in professional debates without holding the slightest grudge or feeling the least bit defensive. Upon meeting Lorentz, one had the feeling that his whole heart and soul were tied up in his life's work of physics. Nothing could distract him from his work or get him derailed from his path of logic. His work was, truly, like a work of art which was planned out to the smallest detail. I have no doubt that he was the greatest Dutch physicist of all time.

BUCKY: You say "Dutch" physicist. Of course many people consider you to be the greatest physicist of any country.

EINSTEIN: My life is a simple thing, really, that would interest no one. There have been many great scientists. I have always admired, for instance, Madame Curie. Not only did she do outstanding work in her lifetime and not only did she help humanity greatly by her work, but she invested all of her work with the highest moral quality. All of this she accomplished with great strength, objectivity and judgment. It is very rare to find all of these qualities in one individual. In fact, if more European intellectuals had had Madame Curie's modesty, conditions there might have been much brighter.

BUCKY: One area that we haven't mentioned is that of politics. Who do you look up to in that realm?

EINSTEIN: Without a doubt, although he didn't actually hold any political office, as such, Gandhi was the greatest political figure of our time. His concept of passive resistance to one's enemies was a great leap in combating war. I consider him, actually, to be the greatest political genius of our time. I think that his current recognition is nowhere near as great as it will be in future generations.

BUCKY: In all of the people to whom you assign the term "greatness," what is it that basically sets off those people from ordinary folk?

EINSTEIN: I think that these great people have to possess a strong

115

urge to understand and to be receptive and creative in all of their worldly dealings. And this brings out another aspect of greatness. That is, that many leaders commonly thought of as great men in many cases have done as much harm to humanity as they have done good. While many common, simple people who are never thought of as great go about their daily business always receptive and creative, but totally unrecognized for it. But these are great people, too. We would be better off, in many cases, if some of these lesser-recognized people took over as political leaders. The absence of people of that caliber helped to make possible the rise of Hitler and Mussolini.

BUCKY: Perhaps the truly great people under those circumstances simply get swallowed up in the mass.

EINSTEIN: Yes, exactly. Unlike one hundred years ago, people today are mostly like sheep. How else can you explain how people, normally peaceful, can within a couple of short weeks, be incited through the well-organized and concentrated efforts of newspaper, television, and radio, to don uniforms and go out and kill or be killed?

BUCKY: What is the solution to such a sad state of affairs?

EINSTEIN: Individuality must be cultivated and respected when it blossoms. One problem is that as population has increased tremendously over the years, the number of outstanding people per capita has declined. Consequently, the leadership has been usurped by organizations, companies, and committees. This, I think, is a sad status. Pooling the resources of many people has, of course, some advantages. But the one large *disadvantage* is that organizations, as such, do not respond to problems with bold thinking, but rather with caution. This is where the individual reigns supreme. But the individuals too easily just hand over their power to the group. This problem is also mirrored in the sciences. The fact that, in general, scientific insights have become limited to a small group of people accounts in part for the weakening of a nation's philosophical thinking and thus contributes to its intellectual decline. In so many ways we are so similar to animals. What happens if a herd of cows are scared? They immediately herd together to form a union. The same with people. Most people when in

116

trouble or in an effort to accomplish some difficult task tend
to either belong to a group or join an organization. Unfortunately, by doing so, most people are completely blinded and
misled. Many times, the views for which they had originally
joined the group change entirely through majority influence.
Others who don't join groups face danger as the ostrich does,
by burying their heads in the sand. However, the ostrich has
more reason to do this than humans, for birds have the
smallest brains of any animals compared to body size. I often
have wondered if the ostrich had a greater amount of brains
would he still bury his head in the sand?

BUCKY: But certainly you are not promoting unbridled individualism?

EINSTEIN: No, no. We must differentiate between individuality
and the cult of the individual. Individuals must seek to excel,
but their subsequent achievements should not be looked upon
as supernatural. Then, too, I do not mean, by criticizing the
group mentality, that people should not feel a strong sense of
community. That is very important, because if a human being
were bereft of community from birth, he would be nothing
but another animal, insofar as thoughts and feelings are concerned. But within that community, an individual can only do
good when his actions are directed toward the promotion of
the good of his fellow man.

BUCKY: This concept of "social responsibility" has always been
very important in your philosophy, hasn't it, Professor?

EINSTEIN: I have always had a passionate sense of social justice
and responsibility, although I must say that it sometimes con-
trasts oddly with my pronounced lack of need for direct
contact with other human beings and human communities. I
have been, I guess you can say, a lone traveler throughout this
life. For instance, I have never really belonged to any country.

BUCKY: So solitude has always been a part of your nature?

EINSTEIN: Yes, I have always, even with close friends, even with
family, had a need to keep a little distance. This was not as easy
in my younger years, but with maturity I find that solitude is so
delicious. And, as well, we have difficulty in old age forming ties
because our faculty of psychological adjustment has declined.

BUCKY: From your mature perspective, then, what advice would you have for modern man to improve his well-being?

EINSTEIN: Just to live as simply as possible. Unfortunately, too many modern luxuries have artificially put our physical organs out of practice, especially the automobile. Could you imagine, when I was a little boy, hiring a carriage to go five blocks to the nearest grocery store to get some things? Yet, this is exactly what people do today. They go into their garage and get in their car to pick up something even only a couple of blocks away. In my earlier days, people got the exercise that nature requires just by virtue of having to walk long distances.

BUCKY: Speaking of a different kind of exercise—mental exercise—I understand that you were close friends with Emanuel Lasker, one of the great masters of chess. You even wrote the introduction to a biography of Lasker. Yet you have said, even in that introduction, that you dislike the game of chess. For what reason, may I ask?

EINSTEIN: For one thing, it is a very competitive game and I do not really enjoy that kind of competition. But the main reason why I do not enjoy the game of chess is an ethical one. And that is because the main goal of the game is to defeat your partner through the use of various types of tricks and deception.

BUCKY: What major changes have you noticed in yourself with the passing of the years?

EINSTEIN: Not very much, really. The only thing that I can think of is that my views on some factual matters have changed compared with how I looked upon them, say, ten years ago. I find this to be a curious matter, for the facts have not changed in those ten years. Therefore, it must be my own psyche that has altered. But, anyway, as I grow older, I realize that man's eternal struggle against death will always be with us. Anyone who is really serious knows that life is only a big adventure.

3. *Conversation with Margot*

In 1986, shortly before her death, Margot Einstein, the step-daughter of Albert Einstein, invited me to have lunch with her and reminisce about old times in his home in Princeton.

I was happy to have that opportunity to share memories with her, and although she was 86 years old at the time, she still maintained a sense of humor and a strong memory about some things.

Fortunately, I decided to carry with me a recorder so that I could prod my own memory later in preparation for writing this book. I say "fortunately" because, as it turned out, this was to be the last record of any comments from Einstein's step-daughter.

The day was also fortuitous because in the middle of our conversations, Dr. Otto Nathan, Einstein's literary executor, walked in. Dr. Nathan had been visiting the family of Jamie Sayen, author of *Einstein in America,* who had just written a memoir of life next door to Einstein—although he himself, was too young to have met Einstein. Dr. Nathan, who was already over 90, died shortly after these talks.

What follows, then, is a transcription of the more significant parts of that day's conversations with Margot Einstein and Otto Nathan. I have only slightly edited the tape to try to reflect the flavor of relaxed congeniality and familiarity that prevailed among us. Occasionally, I have inserted an editorial comment to explain facts that may not be familiar to the reader.

BUCKY: Hello, Margotchen. Please do not get up. I brought you many pictures that I thought you might be interested in.
> [EDITOR'S NOTE: I had brought with me as a means of stimulating conversations and memories a new update of Ronald Clark's biography, *Albert Einstein: The Life and Times,* which had been re-released as a cocktail table book with many additional photographs, some of which had come from, or included, the Bucky family.]

MARGOT: There are so many old pictures in this book!

BUCKY: Let me explain something to you. Many of the pictures in this book, I, myself, gave to the author.

MARGOT: Oh, I see.

BUCKY: You have gained a little weight since the last time I saw you, have you not?

MARGOT: Yes, I'm afraid so.

BUCKY: Well, that's a good sign. It means that you are healthy.

MARGOT: Oh, here is my picture, too.

BUCKY: Yes, with Ilse. There are many pictures of Ilse.
[EDITOR'S NOTE: Ilse, of course, was Margot's sister, who had died more than fifty years earlier.]

MARGOT: This was so very kind of you to bring this book. Thank you so much.

BUCKY: Does Helen Dukas's sister ever visit you?

MARGOT: Yes, she comes once a year. She comes for lunch, but she likes to come more in the spring.

BUCKY: So, Margot, how do you feel these days?

MARGOT: I tell you, I am well, but of course, I am also old now. Sure, that makes me much more tired, in my mind, in my head, you know.

BUCKY: You say you are old, but your father invented a word— that is, "relative." So, you see, your age is only relative.

MARGOT: Well, it is relative. I noticed that in my aunts. I am not as grouchy as some people are. Every morning I go with the girl for a walk, and if I am not too tired, I also go in the afternoon.

BUCKY: So, then, you still take your walks, after all these years!

MARGOT: Oh, sure. My walking is very good, only my memory is not quite the same. But still, it is not too bad. I do not know any more too many people in Princeton, as most of my friends were in the former generation, and they have all mostly died out. The only ones left of my father's friends are you and Mr. Nathan. My father would be 108 years old today, can you imagine?

BUCKY: Do you remember Ilse?

MARGOT: Yes, of course. Poor Ilse, she died so young. I believe she had tuberculosis much earlier than the doctors discovered. She was very frail, but as a young girl, she was the picture of health. I remember how old my mother became when Ilse died.

BUCKY: Was Ilse happily married to Rudy?

MARGOT: Yes, sure, sure.

BUCKY: Did Rudy's second wife ever visit you?

> [EDITOR'S NOTE: Rudolph Kayser, the husband of Ilse, married my own former girlfriend, Eva, after Ilse's death.]

MARGOT: Eva? Of course, we were very close. She was a very intelligent person.

BUCKY: But, then, after Rudy died, she never got married again?

MARGOT: No, Eva did not marry again.

BUCKY: Is she still teaching?

> [EDITOR'S NOTE: Eva Kayser had been for some time teaching French in a school in New York City.]

MARGOT: I don't think so, but I think that she occasionally writes, and is still living in New York. I really can't be sure, as I am so forgetful in old age.

BUCKY: But, Dr. Nathan has a good memory. He remembers more than me; for example, he gave me very detailed directions how to get here from New York.

MARGOT: Well, I can't change it. You know that is the nature of old age. I also notice that one is more slow and the incentive for work is not there any more. But as long as I can take my walks, I am very glad.

BUCKY: Well, your father, too, he took walks until the end. He loved to walk.

MARGOT: Albert was a very good walker.

BUCKY: Yes, he loved to walk. He even walked in bad weather. By the way, whatever happened to your father's boat?

MARGOT: That I could not tell you.

BUCKY: Have you ever met Mileva?

> [EDITOR'S NOTE: This, of course, refers to Einstein's first wife.]

MARGOT: Yes, I did, but I have a very short memory. She came once to visit us in the Haberlandstrasse in Berlin, and she was very kind and nice with me.

BUCKY: Yes. Were they very friendly even after the divorce?

MARGOT: Yes, but for him to be married to her was very hard for him, because I think that she was a bit of a psychopath. But she was a very intelligent person.

BUCKY: What happened to Hans Albert's children?

MARGOT: This I do not know.

BUCKY: Do you remember your other father?

MARGOT: No, only from pictures.

BUCKY: What did your real father do?

MARGOT: He was a merchant.

BUCKY: I understand that Dr. Nathan is next door visiting your neighbor, whose son is writing the book about Einstein.

MARGOT: Yes, they are very nice people and so is the son.

> [EDITOR'S NOTE: At this time, Dr. Nathan walked in from next door and sat in on the rest of our conversation.]

MARGOT (to Otto): Peter's parent's were wonderful people. Always, people could come to them to have lunch at any time without any previous announcements. It was a meeting place for all refugees coming from Europe.

BUCKY: I will tell you a true story that will prove Margot's point about the refugees all coming to the Buckys for lunch. A refugee who was in the U.S.A. went to Paris and he met a refugee who was himself on his way to the United States. So the refugee heading for America said to the other one, "I am worried about how I can get started in the U.S.A. I don't have much money and I don't know how I am going to be able to live there. What should I do?" So the refugee who was on his way back from the U.S.A. told the man, "It is very simple. When you get to New York, all you have to do is call Dr. Bucky."

MARGOT: Yes [laughing]. Your father was sometimes like a naughty boy.

BUCKY: He always was a naughty boy, and he liked puzzles. Do you remember this?

MARGOT: Oh, yes, he was a lovely person, that is true, and he had so many jokes, and he liked to play them also.

BUCKY: I will tell you another story. Once Albert Einstein was over for dinner in our place in New York. At that time, he had been placed on a special diet. We all had a wonderful dinner that my mother served, but when it came time for dessert, everybody was served a luscious cake. Since my mother knew about Einstein's special diet, she had made him a custom-made soft dessert that he was able to eat. But when the places had been set for dinner, everyone had been given a cake fork. When my mother noticed this, she quickly arose and said to Albert, "Don't worry, I will get you a spoon." But Albert waved her off, saying, "No, no, no." Then he took the fork and ate his soft dessert with the handle. Yes, I remember a lot of things. Were you in Watch Hill, Rhode Island, that one summer with us?

MARGOT: Where Albert fell out of the boat, or what?

BUCKY: Albert did once fall out of his boat. Did you know this? You know, he could not swim. And he was hanging out of the boat when we came, holding on for dear life. When we arrived, he said, "I must get credit for this bath!" Also, we could not convince him to get an emergency motor in his sailboat. Once, in Watch Hill, I don't know whether you remember, he was not home yet from sailing at ten o'clock at night.

MARGOT: Yes, I know, and my mother was shouting so loud!

BUCKY: And we sent the Coast Guard out to get him, but when they found him, he was not the slightest bit worried, and he said, "The wind has to come sometime!"

MARGOT: What else could he do. He had no other choice.

BUCKY: He was also against life preservers. But, finally, my father succeeded in giving him a pillow to sit on, which also could double as a life preserver in case of danger. Did you ever see the movies I took of him?

MARGOT: No.

BUCKY: In his first house in Princeton, I took a movie, and he thumbed his hand at the camera.

MARGOT: How is your wife keeping?

BUCKY: Very well. Do you know that she was half my age when I married her. She was twenty-four and I was forty-eight. But I passed my parole. I am married to her twenty-four years. But now she is creeping up. The older she gets, the closer she gets, you know?

NATHAN: Now you have given yourself away, because that means you are now seventy-two.

BUCKY: Dr. Nathan, your head is still intact, because you can still do mathematics, but please don't broadcast my age. You know what my secret is? I do not smoke, and I do not drink, but I only look at pretty girls.

MARGOT: So, you have no vices, then?

BUCKY: Oh, yes, I have vices. I am a born gambler. I love slot machines, and Atlantic City is so close now. You know, I am the only person who goes to Atlantic City and makes a profit, as I have equipped three casinos with security X-ray units for bombs and loaded dice.

MARGOT: I remember, Peterchen, you had a good time when you were younger and you had plenty of girlfriends. Albert told me all about it, and he liked some of them, too. And the cars you had—I remember the Thunderbird with all of the musical horns.

BUCKY: That reminds me. I want to tell you a funny but true story about the Thunderbird. I only had the car for about two weeks when it was stolen. That same day, when the car was stolen, I received a telephone call from the police precinct in Greenwich Village that they had found the car. I went there to claim it and found that no damage was done. As I drove the car home, a motorcycle policeman stopped me and asked me for the registration for the car. I did not have it with me, so I was arrested for stealing my own car, because the police out on the road still had the report out that the car had been stolen!

Margot, I want to give you the son of Chico!

[EDITOR'S NOTE: My reference to the "Son of Chico," of course, was only symbolic, since I only meant to make a present to Margot of a similar wire-haired terrier.]

MARGOT: No, no . . . I don't want any animal to love now because there are now so many cars that pass by on the street outside. If I had birds and they would fly away, that is fine. I like to see the birds come and eat out of our birdfeeders and then fly away. You know, Peterchen, I am so glad that you came. It really feels like old times again. I loved to be with your parents, and especially your mother, who I considered like my own mother. Albert told us so many times how much he liked you and your parents—which, by the way, he didn't say of too many people. The reason he said that was because your father was a simple man like he was, uncomplicated and not false.

124

What Albert liked most of all about you and your family, though, was the fact that you tried to protect him from people, as others always wanted to show off with him by presenting him as if on a golden platter.

BUCKY: Have you heard from Thomas lately?

    [EDITOR'S NOTE: I was referring here to my own brother, Thomas Bucky, a physician who was living in Connecticut.]

MARGOT: No, he has not been here for a long time. We are very upset with what he has done lately.

BUCKY: What was that?

MARGOT: I don't want to tell you in detail, but he has hurt us all very deeply lately when he sold an item that Albert gave him as a present, which Albert treasured very much. I am so glad that Albert is not alive to have witnessed this, as it would have made him very sad. But Albert also told us many times that his happiest times were when he could tinker with your father in his laboratory in New York.

BUCKY: So Thomas has never called you?

MARGOT: I don't remember. I remember your father so well. He was always so witty.

BUCKY: Yes, he was. When he first met my wife, he liked her very much and do you know what he liked to call people he liked? Stupid! In other words, if we would come to visit him, he would call, "Tina, how are you, Stupid?" She, of course, at first didn't know what to say, but soon realized that it was meant as a friendly greeting. Tina was the only girl of the many that I went out with that my father approved of, and he liked her very much.

MARGOT: All of these things are years and years ago, and I don't always remember. But I remember your father clearly.

    I was many times in my life so deadly sick that they gave me up, but I always came back.

BUCKY: Do you remember when you took the trips to Europe to recuperate? And to Switzerland and many other countries?

MARGOT: Yes. You know it is very strange. When one gets old there just seems to be a curtain over everything.

BUCKY: That is very good.

MARGOT: What do you mean?

BUCKY: You do not want to remember all of the bad things. You could not go on in life if you did not forget.

MARGOT: Well, I must say, my memory has suffered very much.

BUCKY: Well, one thing that doesn't seem to have changed much is your telephone number. It is still the same as it was 50 years ago—1606. And also, Princeton itself does not seem to have changed much, except for one thing. And I am sorry that your father could not have seen this change as he would have liked it very much: that is, that Princeton University now has girl students.

Do you miss Helen Dukas since she passed away?

MARGOT: Oh, yes, very much. You know she knew and had to know everything, and I did not.

BUCKY: You know, we had a different name for Miss Dukas. We called her "the living dictionary."

MARGOT: Yes, that is so true. She had a very good memory. But I remember so well your parents with so many people there at their house.

BUCKY: Yes, they were always helping refugees.

MARGOT: Always so kind and every day, the big luncheon for the refugees. Dr. Bucky always treated me too and gave me grenz rays.

BUCKY: Did he help you?

MARGOT: Yes, it did help very much.

BUCKY: And I drove your father so many times.

MARGOT: Yes, I know. He was always so grateful for you.

BUCKY: He even dedicated a picture to me, "To Peter Bucky, the Automobile Driver." Were you in Watch Hill that summer with us?

MARGOT: Yes, I was there.

BUCKY: Do you remember, while we were there, I built this big short-wave radio station so that your father could listen to Hitler and all of the Nazis over the radio?

MARGOT: I don't remember that, but I remember you very well as a young man.

BUCKY: You mean with my car with all of the musical horns?

MARGOT: Yes. I am so tired in my head today, you must excuse me. You know I suffer so much during a weather change on account of my sinuses. I am more or less used to it, but then I am not so good in my mind.

BUCKY: Yes, that is why you went to Europe, on account of your sinus trouble, wasn't it?

MARGOT: Yes. I don't complain about it in general, but it makes my head so tired and this I do not like.

> [EDITOR'S NOTE: At this point, Mrs. Sayens, Jamie's mother, walked into the room. She had been conversing in another room with Dr. Nathan about her son's book.]

BUCKY (to Mrs. Sayens): Has your son ever met Professor Einstein?

MRS. SAYENS: No, we did not move next door until after 1955. My son is a writer and his field is history.

BUCKY: Margot, do you ever watch television?

MARGOT: No, only if there is something about animals, because this is what I like.

BUCKY: Do you remember my baby, Chico?

MARGOT: Oh, Chico, that was my dog. Oh, how I loved Chico. He was buried in our back yard here. I believe he was twelve years old when he died.

4. Einstein's Roving Eye

Albert Einstein was fortunate that he lived in a more discreet age than our present era of kiss-and-tell. Affairs of the heart, unlike today, were generally handled with discretion by the news media, with the possible exception of juicy Hollywood scandals, which were, after all, expected by the public. But famous people of great accomplishments were treated with kid gloves as far as their private lives were concerned, leaving their public reputations intact. Thus, only several decades after actual events did the public learn of the affairs of such public figures as Franklin Roosevelt, Walter Lippman, Dwight Eisenhower, or John F. Kennedy.

While Albert Einstein presented an avuncular image to the public—the shaggy-haired, soft-spoken, congenial "everybody's uncle"—there is no doubt that the greatest scientist of our century would have graced the pages of some of our less reputable sensationalist newspapers had he lived in our less discreet age. For, as much as it might surprise those who view Einstein as the ultimate "absent-minded professor," he was still a man with a keen appreciation of the female sex. Indeed, it can be truthfully said that Albert Einstein had a "roving eye" that occasionally got him into domestic troubles.

When the *New York Times* broke the story on Sunday, 3 May 1987 informing the world that Einstein and his fellow physics student Mileva Maric had conceived and brought into the world an illegitimate daughter, born in early 1902, a full year before the couple's subsequent marriage, it came as no surprise to those of us who knew the Einsteins intimately. Though Einstein never spoke to me about his having sired a daughter, his passionate nature and his weakness for pretty women were no secret to me. In fact, those of us who knew the Einsteins in their younger days in Berlin and Caputh can recall many circumstances when his second wife, Elsa, was at her wit's end over Einstein's open flirtations.

It is nothing new in the annals of marriage that men have often gone astray and sometimes have in the process been either foolish or careless enough to get caught by their spouses. What was unusual in Einstein's case was the fact that he was unconventional enough to practically flaunt his peccadilloes in his wife's face.

In Germany, there was an attractive and wealthy widow named Toni Mendel who lived in a suburb of Berlin called Wannsee. Mrs. Mendel had made Einstein's acquaintance and soon inserted herself into his life. She made a habit of bringing him candy (another unconventional twist on the normal wooing pattern of the man showering his object of affection with candy and flowers). Mrs. Mendel shared a love for the theater with Einstein, and she would often invite him to plays. She, being wealthy, would pay for the tickets and send for Einstein in a limousine.

In fact, I was visiting the Einstein home once when the physicist was preparing for one of these dates and I remember a big fight ensuing over the fact that Elsa would not give Albert any money. I recall Einstein shouting, "If I am invited to the theater and someone calls for me in a limousine, I at least want to have enough money with me to pay for the hatcheck girl!"

As can be expected, Elsa was not very enthusiastic about this, especially as Einstein often did not come home from these jaunts until early the next morning. But, despite Elsa's disapproval, Einstein's and Mrs. Mendel's relationship persisted. In fact, at one time, a large body of correspondence between Einstein and Toni Mendel existed, but later, upon Einstein's wish, these letters were burned. (It is possible that one of these letters may have slipped away, however. In a *New York Post* column in 1982, a letter was quoted as being for sale by the Nevada Historical Documents Museum in Las Vegas, Nevada. The letter was purportedly from Einstein to an unnamed mistress—who might very well have been Toni Mendel, since the letter was written by hand in the German language. In the letter, Einstein writes: "Liebchen . . . I work hard, and in the meantime I think happily of you. . . . This letter is written under great difficulty, as Else [sic] may come at any moment, and so I really have to watch. . . . Yesterday was so beautiful that I am still filled with delight. . . . I will come again 5 o'clock at the same place, or better still, ten minutes before five if you can arrange it. . . . Be kissed, my dear, from your A.E.")

Often, too, a young lady from Austria would accompany Einstein during his sailing in Caputh. She came to the house there about once a week and would bring Viennese confections that, ironically, Elsa enjoyed. Whenever she came to the house to sail, Mrs. Einstein would leave in the morning to shop in Berlin and would not return until very late. Before leaving, she would sometimes announce to her daughters, "Now I have cleared the field for him!"

But Elsa was not quite as understanding as this might indicate. There were many violent arguments over these women and Elsa was often so saddened by the situation that she wept. But both of her daughters, trying to keep a perspective on things, advised their mother that she would either have to leave Einstein or learn to tolerate this aspect of his life and character.

One of his closest friends in Berlin was the architect Conrad Wachsmann. Wachsmann, who designed the Einsteins' summer home in Caputh, was treated so much like a member of the family that he was often present during their arguments. Often, Elsa would confront Wachsmann to dare him to take a side in their argument (to her chagrin, I might add, as invariably, Wachsmann would see things Albert's way, to which Elsa would retort, "Oh, you men all stick together!"). Wachsmann once said, "I liked the idea that Einstein treated me like a son, but he could also be very strict—like a father." But as a result of his closeness to the Einsteins, he was able to add some insights into both Albert Einstein's philosophy of women and Elsa's personal feelings of heartbreak over Einstein's occasional wanderings.

Once, when Wachsmann was visiting he brought along a casual girlfriend but was shy about introducing her since he knew that he might never see her again. But Einstein allayed his fears, telling him: "That shouldn't make any difference to you. And even if you bring two girlfriends along, I wouldn't be angry. It is a wonderful privilege of youth that they will never be punished because they don't always eat out of the same pot, which they are not forced to do."

Wachsmann told of another, more sensitive occasion. He had attempted to visit the Einsteins in their Berlin apartment, but was turned away by the doorman, who insisted to Wachsmann that the Einsteins were away at Caputh. Suddenly Elsa appeared and invited him upstairs. Wachsmann knew right away that something was wrong, and she quickly confirmed this, confessing that she was always very lonely, as Albert was in Caputh, sailing with his Austrian lady friend.

Elsa offered Wachsmann some cognac, which was very unusual for her. She then joined him in a drink, which quickly made her giddily talkative. She reminisced about her early years with Einstein. But she quickly became more melancholy as she told Wachsmann how hurt she was because Einstein was always looking at beautiful women. She asked Wachsmann whether or not he thought her pretty.

"You are as pretty as a rose," Wachsmann responded, reaching for Elsa's hand to kiss it. "But a rose does not always stay as a budding rose. But people still like older roses because even when they get older, they still remain beautiful."

Elsa replied, "My dear Conrad, I don't believe you. Why does Professor Einstein show so much interest in other women?"

Wachsmann answered, "You must visualize the professor as being in a garden of roses. So that he may be sure that he has the nicest rose, he has to check out all the other roses."

Wachsmann reported that Elsa seemed to be partly convinced by his little parable and told him, "That was very nicely said." But Wachsmann left soon after this, as he was too embarrassed at having to answer Elsa's questions.

One can also get an inkling of Einstein's ideas on monogamy and faithfulness from a letter he wrote to an anxious lady friend who had written complaining that her own husband had not been true to her and asking for Einstein's advice. Einstein wrote back, "You probably know that most men, the same as most women, do not have a monogamous nature. These people act even much stronger if there are any obstacles put in their way to keep them from doing what they feel like doing. To force a person to be true is, for everybody concerned, a very bitter fruit."

It would seem that Einstein might very well have been looking to his own personal experience in responding to his friend's letter. Aside from his apparent dalliances in Berlin, and his premarital experience with Mileva Maric in Switzerland, it has up until now been unknown to the general public that Einstein may have carried on a long-standing affair with his secretary of twenty-eight years, Helen Dukas.

On many occasions, Einstein's son Hans Albert told me and my wife, Tina, of his long-held suspicion of this affair. And there is some circumstantial evidence that points strongly to such a liaison.

First, of course, was the death of Einstein's second wife, Elsa, in 1936, which left Einstein alone for the final nineteen years of his life in Princeton. Helen Dukas, herself unmarried, lived in the Einstein home for all of these years. Partly, Hans Albert's suspicions were fed by the fact that Miss Dukas's bedroom had been conveniently situated directly off of Einstein's own study, where he spent a good part of his evenings and nights.

But an even more strongly indicative factor is to be found in Einstein's will. It was drafted while his beloved sister, step-daughter, two sons, and grandson were all alive, and still showed a strong favoritism for Miss Dukas.

For example, while Einstein bequeathed to his son Eduard the sum of fifteen thousand dollars; to his son Hans Albert the sum of ten thousand dollars; to his sister, Maja, the sum of ten thousand dollars, held in trust by Margot—in comparison with these bequests he willed twenty thousand dollars to Helen Dukas. This was the same as the amount he willed to his own step-daughter, with whom he had lived for two decades.

Not only was Miss Dukas's bequeathal on a grand scale, but Einstein also made her the sole beneficiary of the trust fund he set up to collect the royalties and investments from royalties on any of his literary properties as long as she should live (which, in the event, turned out to be twenty-seven years after his death). This while his step-daughter Margot would have better benefitted, living as she did for thirty-two years after Einstein's death.

Indeed, there would seem to be more to this than the grateful generosity of an employer to a secretary who had served him well. Perhaps, then, Hans Albert's intuition was correct.

Strangely, there may be an even more bizarre explanation for Einstein's generosity and devotion to Helen Dukas. Recalling the bombshell that was let out in 1987 with publication of Einstein's letters to his first wife, the reader will remember that for the first time, the world was informed of the existence of an illegitimate daughter born to Einstein and Miss Maric prior to their marriage.

But, as the *New York Times* reported on 3 May 1987. "The fate of the child, a girl, however, remains a mystery. She was born before the couple married and there apparently is no record of what became of her. She apparently never lived with the Einsteins."

The same article reported that the girl spent some time with Mileva's mother in Yugoslavia and suffered a bout of scarlet fever, from which she recovered. "The mention of scarlet fever is the last reference to the girl in the correspondence," it said. "Whether the girl was being reared by Miss Maric's family, had been adopted, or met some other fate remains unknown."

When Helen Dukas's obituary was published in the *New York Times* on 14 February 1982, despite other extensive details no mention was made of any life prior to her coming to work in 1927 in Germany. This is highly unusual for a newspaper that prides itself on being "the newspaper of record." It may be explainable, of course, by a dearth of information about Miss Dukas prior to 1927.

The only mention of her life prior to working for Einstein in 1927 in the major Einstein biographies cites her as having been referred to him by her "sister," a Rosa Dukas, who was the executive secretary of the Jewish Orphans Organization in Berlin. Rosa suggested that Helen would fit the bill as a secretary for Einstein, who because of medical problems needed some organizational assistance.

That is the official story. However, it does strike one as odd that a young woman of Helen's intelligence would have totally forsaken a life of her own to follow Einstein across the Atlantic Ocean and to live in his home, indeed, to continue to reside there for nearly three decades past Einstein's death. One cannot help but wonder, therefore, whether there is another explanation besides sheer dedication. Consider, then, the following scenario:

An illegitimate daughter is born to Albert Einstein and Mileva Maric in early 1902. Because of Einstein's parents' hostility to Miss Maric and because of general societal proscriptions against illegitimate children, the couple must give their daughter up to be reared apart from them. Even after marrying, Einstein's impending fame proscribes a revelation of the "ill-begotten" child.

From this point, the girl is either (1) given over to an organization (the Jewish Orphans Organization, run by Rosa Dukas?), or (2) adopted into another family (perhaps the Dukas family, one that was very involved with orphan and unwanted children?). Later, prompted either by an adopted child's frantic search for her true parents or by Einstein's chance rediscovery of his missing daughter, the two are rejoined.

The girl, now called Helen Dukas, is perfectly suited to deal with the technical requirements of organizing Einstein's work. In her genetic make-up are, after all, the seeds of science, having sprung from both the greatest physicist of the twentieth century and his physicist girl friend. So a cover story is easily contrived and Einstein's long-lost daughter, Helen Dukas, comes to work for him, ends up serving and living with him for the rest of his life— and takes her rightful place, as Einstein's first-born, in his will as his major beneficiary. As Dr. Otto Nathan remarked upon Miss Dukas's death: "Einstein died a second death when she died."

Fact or fiction? Lover or daughter? Or just dedicated secretary whom he recognized for her devotion with his beneficence? Perhaps we will never know. But one thing is certain: Those who knew the real Einstein, the man behind the public facade, were aware of his humanity, with both the bright and the dark sides that that term implies.

Einstein, in other words, was not a caricature of himself—the absent-minded professor with his head in the clouds, as he was so often depicted. Rather, he was planted firmly in the realities of life.

I recall once, in my younger days, when Cupid's arrow had pierced my own heart. Unfortunately, the object of my affections, a girl named Virginia, did not meet with my mother's approval, which caused a considerable amount of friction in our home.

In the course of socializing with us, Einstein became aware of this little conflict between mother and son. One day, after he had returned to Princeton, a letter arrived in our mail, bearing the Princeton postmark. Included in the envelope was a page on which Einstein had composed a poem written on the subject of our family clash. It read as follows:

ELEGY, TO BE SUNG IN TWO PARTS .
BY MASTER PETER AND HIS MOMMY

Today I am sending you a poem
It is not by Schiller, you can guess.
It does not soar proudly in the air
And its fragrance is very down-to-earth.

Virginia is dangerous
She does it sweetly and also cleverly.
Mother, on the other hand,
Excels in watchfulness.

We do not envy Master Peter . . .
The way he is handled by these two.
He twists and turns the best he can
As a strong man should.

Anyone ever stuck like this
Has respect for such a thing.
He knows how helpless and confused
Menfolk are in such a fix.

Fury docs not achieve a thing
In delicate matters such as this.
One is plucked and tormented.
But courage! Time heals such wounds.

And the moral of the story
(Which one hardly ever discusses)
Is that the upper half plans and thinks
While the lower half determines our fate.

As Dennis Overbye wrote in a recent *Time Magazine* essay: "Einstein was an ordinary man. He could see past space and time, yes, but not sex. . . . So let us not mourn the loss of a plaster saint. . . . The man who had the great thoughts and spun the strange theories that inspired that veneration was young, full of vigor and turbulence and passion. He was hardly alone; all his organs worked as well as his brain. His household was squirming with babies when he began his greatest work. . . . Einstein's physics flourished not in the absence of life but in its fullness. His scientific life blossomed at the same time as the rest of his life. When he was in love."

CHAPTER EIGHT

Einstein the Poet

A Selection of Light-Hearted Poetry

The little poem that I quoted near the end of the last chapter is an example of an aspect of Einstein's playful mind—his penchant for organizing his thoughts into light verse. Not much has been written about this. Only an occasional citation in various biographies makes mention of the little doggerels that Einstein scattered throughout his life among friends, correspondents, and organizations.

But Einstein did, indeed, produce many of these ditties, often responding to advice-seekers or to friends' problems with a few pertinent quatrains. I have jotted down on occasion poems written by Albert Einstein that I have come across, either from our family's correspondence or from various other media. For the first time, then, in one printed source, I would like to offer readers a sampling of "Einstein the poet," proving once again that his was, indeed, a multi-faceted talent.

The poem that closed the last chapter was not the first example of Einstein's using verse to try to cajole my family out of despondency. Once, when my brother, Thomas, was sent by his doctors to the mountains to recuperate from a bout of tuberculosis, Einstein sent him the following poem to try to lift his spirits:

> In the city everyone sighs
> For peace and quiet
> And wants to escape the tumult
> For the mountains and the sky.
>
> You are required to take
> What others vainly seek—
> The view, free and wide,
> And tranquil solitude.

Sometimes Einstein composed a poem simply to extol one of his intellectual heroes, as he did in this small tribute to the great Spinoza, written in 1920:

> Oh, how I love this noble soul
> More than words can e'er extol.
> I fear though he'll remain alone
> With shining halo of his own.

In the height of the panic that spread throughout the Jewish community as Hitler's forces gained power, Einstein was expelled from the Prussian Academy of Sciences for "spreading atrocity stories about Germany." He retorted with a few concise thoughts in verse, which he addressed to the Academy on 7 April 1933:

> Whoever writes grim fairy tales
> Will end up in our harshest jails.
> But if he dares the truth to tell
> We'll cast his soul down into hell.
>
> Courageous are we now and then
> When danger doesn't threaten,
> But when the mob begins to rage
> We sometimes lose our courage.

Once, after receiving a particularly heavy delivery of mail from his admiring public, Einstein took pen to paper to record his feelings of mock despair, as he did here:

> The postman brings me every day
> Piles of mail to my dismay.
> Oh, why does no one ever reason
> That he is one while we are legion.

One of Einstein's assistants once presented him with a page of calculations upon which he had worked out with great care a formulation that Einstein immediately discovered to have been flawed. Rather than hurt his assistant's feelings with a direct confrontation, Einstein returned the page of calculations, upon which he had superimposed this little ditty:

> It's easy to say something new
> If all sense one will eschew,
> But hardly is it ever found
> That the new is also sound.

Einstein believed deeply that his stubborn persistence in problem-solving was what caused him to succeed, rather than any incipient "greatness." To illustrate this, he once inscribed a book of essays about his science and philosophy with this two-liner:

> One can clearly see herein
> Just what stubbornness can win.

In 1938, after a jointly-authored book (with Leopold Infeld: *The Evolution of Physics*) was assailed by Nazi scientists, Einstein responded with an allegory about a lark and a dung-beetle:

> The lark trills on a sunny day.
> Dung beetle listens with dismay.
> "Your sing-song is a rotten jest,"
> He proclaims with swollen chest.

> "I'll only greet those men who keep
> Their feet aground without a peep,
> And what I cannot understand,
> Is nonsense—I'm the cleverest man!"

> Skylarks warble their songs in May,
> Ignoring what the beetles say,
> "If the song disturbs your slumber,
> Plug your ears and you'll grow number."

Einstein abhorred social functions such as fund-raising dinners, and after his wife died he increasingly refused invitations to them. In 1936, in response to one such invitation, he composed the following RSVP:

> Alas, one is reminded daily
> That endless dining goes on gaily
> So fools might make a large donation
> What a needless aggravation!

Gorge yourself voraciously,
All alone, sagaciously.
Whoever knows how to do this
Has found the path to mortal bliss.

Next to his contributions to science, Einstein was probably best known as an amateur violinist. Many musicians who joined him for an evening of music-making often came away with plaudits for his skills, calling him a very sensitive violinist. But as in other areas of his life, he could occasionally be self-deprecating about his talents as a fiddler, as in this light verse:

Just because one loves to fiddle,
It's still not right to try and diddle
About your skills to other folks
Or you'll become the butt of jokes.

Still, the dilettante has the right
To scratch and scrape all through the night;
But so his neighbors do not mutter
He must kindly close the shutter.

Einstein admired President Franklin Roosevelt and often bemoaned the fact that Roosevelt's presiding over the war precluded the two men's becoming greater friends. After staying overnight in the White House on 24 January 1934, Einstein wrote a small verse to express his feelings:

In the Capital's proud magnificence
Where destiny is made
Cheerfully fights a proud man
Who can provide the solution.

In our conversation of last night
There were cordial thoughts of you
Which must be spoken
So I send this greeting.

In 1933, on a visit to New York City, Einstein and his wife became godparents of the son of the managing director of the Jewish

Telegraphic Agency. On the back of a photograph of himself, he inscribed this ditty:

TO LITTLE ALBERT LANDAU ON THE
OCCASION OF HIS ENTERING THE WORLD

If others often plague thee
Or do or say evil of thee,
Think also they came here
Without having asked for it.

Think, though you may not like it,
You, too, plagued others often.
As this cannot be altered,
Think gently of everyone.

There is at least one recorded instance of one of Einstein's verses landing him a distinguished position. In 1931 he had traveled to England, where he took part in some scientific colloquiums at Christ Church, Oxford. Some of the regulars at Christ Church hoped that this might signal a more permanent connection between Einstein and the college, while others were averse to allowing an unclubby sort, let alone a German Jew, into the college. But, thanks to a discovery of R.H. Dundas, a resident of Christ Church whose rooms Einstein had used during his stay there, a considerable amount of internal support was drummed up for offering him the position of "Student of Christ Church" (the equivalent of "Fellow" in other schools), which he gratefully accepted. The discovery that Dundas made was of a charming poem that Einstein had left in his host's visitor's book. It went like this:

Dundas lets his rooms decay
While he lingers far away,
Drinking wisdom at the source
Where the sun begins its course.

That his walls may not grow cold
He's installed a hermit old,
One that undeterredly preaches
What the art of numbers teaches.

Shelves of towering folios
Meditate in solemn rows;
Find it strange that one can dwell
Here without their aid so well.

Grumble: Why's this creature staying
With his pipe and piano-playing?
Why should this barbarian roam?
Could he not have stopped at home?

Often though his thoughts will stray
To the owner far away,
Hoping one day face to face
To behold him in this place

With hearty thanks and greetings. —1931

On the occasion of his fiftieth birthday in Berlin Einstein was showered with gifts and congratulations from all over the world. For this occasion, he composed a doggerel, which he mimeographed and mailed as a general note of thanks to all of his benefactors. And while the rhyme is lost in translation, the spirit is worthy of repeating:

Everyone shows their best face today,
And from near and far have sweetly written,
Showering me with all things one could wish for
That still matter to an old man.
Everyone approaches with nice voices
In order to make a better day of it,
And even the innumerable spongers have paid their tribute.
And so I feel lifted up like a noble eagle.
Now the day nears its close and I send you my compliments.
Everything that you did was good, and the sun smiles.

Einstein was a personal friend to Queen Elizabeth of Belgium and often corresponded with her. On occasion, this correspondence took the form of light poems, such as when, writing from Santa Barbara, California, he sent the Queen the following quatrain with a small twig from a tree that she had planted on a previous visit:

In cloister garden a small tree stands.
Planted by your very hands.
It sends—its greetings to convey—
A twig, for it, itself, must stay.
—2/19/33

The Queen responded in kind less than a month later in a ditty that played upon the phrase "One Stone"—the English translation of "Ein Stein":

The twig the greeting did convey
From the tree that had to stay
And from the friend, whose heart so big,
Could send great joy by tiny twig.

A thousand thanks aloud I cry
Unto mountain, sea, and sky.
Now, when stones begin to shake,
I pray *one stone* no harm will take.

For another birthday celebration—this time, his seventieth birthday—in 1949, the German author and playwright Sam Groneman had written Einstein some verses honoring him and claiming him as one of Israel's own. Einstein promptly wrote back with his own verse:

Non-comprehenders are often distressed.
Not you, though—because with good humor you're blessed.
After all, your thought went like this, I dare say:
It was none but the Lord who made us that way.

The Lord takes revenge—and it's simply unfair,
For he himself made the weakness we bear.
And lacking defense, we succumb to this badness,
Sometimes in triumph, and sometimes in sadness.

But rather than stubbornly uttering curses,
You bring us salvation by means of your verses,
Which are cunningly made so the just and the sinners
End up by counting themselves all as winners.

142

As I noted in other sections of this book, Einstein was extremely averse to publicity of any kind and was very shy about the sorts of throngs that would crowd around him, seeking autographs at public places. He once addressed this issue below a photograph of himself that he sent to an old friend, Mrs. Cornelia Wolf, in 1927:

> Wherever I go and wherever I stay,
> There's always a picture of me on display.
> On top of the desk, or out in the hall,
> Tied round a neck, or hung on the wall.
>
> Women and men, they play a strange game,
> Asking, beseeching: "Please sign your name."
> From the erudite fellow they brook not a quibble,
> But firmly insist on a piece of his scribble.
>
> Sometimes, surrounded by all this good cheer,
> I'm puzzled by some of the things that I hear,
> And wonder, my mind for a moment not hazy,
> If I and not they could really be crazy.

One of Einstein's intellectual heroes was Sir Isaac Newton. There exists an undated quatrain that Einstein might have written in 1942, the year of the 300th anniversary of Newton's birth, in which one great scientist three centuries removed pays homage to another:

> Look to the heavens, and learn from them
> How one should really honor the master.
> The stars in their courses extol Newton's laws—
> In silence eternal.

After a Soviet scientist attacked Einstein's theory of relativity as being contrary to the Soviets' faith in dialectical materialism, he vented his anger in the following poem:

WISDOM OF DIALECTICAL MATERIALISM

> By sweat and toil unparalleled
> At last a grain of truth to see?
> Oh fool! To work yourself to death,
> *Our* Party makes the truth by decree.

Does some brave spirit dare to doubt?
A bashed-in skull's his quick reward.
Thus teach we him, as ne'er before,
To live with us in sweet accord.

Einstein was as ready to cast a mirthful stanza at himself as he was otherwise to be the butt of his own jokes. For example, to a photograph sent to a close friend late in life Einstein attached these lines:

Here's what the old guy looks like now.
You feel: This horror my peace will shatter.
Think: What's important is inside.
And anyway—what does it matter?

Einstein often liked to compose quick two-line rhymes to inscribe on photographs sent to friends. On one such picture, taken in Philadelphia, in which he was unaccustomedly dressed in a suit and tie, Einstein wrote:

Although I sit here and stretch my feet out,
It wasn't at home; of that there's no doubt.

To his violinist friend, Boris Schwartz, and his son, with whom Einstein had enjoyed many evenings of chamber music, he once inscribed on a snapshot taken during one of their performances this two-line poem:

To the father and his lad
The playing was—not bad!

On another occasion, the lithographer Emil Orlik captured the essence of Einstein playing his violin, in the process showing the nearly fifty-year-old physicist to have attained a modicum of girth that often dogs those of that mature age. When he saw the lithograph, he wrote to Orlik in another concise two-liner:

For science *something* can be said.
No violinist is so well-fed.

Only two years before his death, Einstein still evinced a delight with words and a playfulness unusual in a man of seventy-four, when, upon viewing a bronze bust by the sculptor Gina Plunguian, he penned the following lines:

> In thought to be absorbed, to strain
> And to overtax the brain
> Not everyone will undertake
> If at all he can escape.
>
> So instead look at this image
> It shows what one can see and grasp.
> Be quite free with blame and praise.
> It can't be heard from far away.

Einstein did not always write his verse out of a spirit of levity or irony. Nor was he always self-mocking. For example, in 1923, obviously in a dark mood, he wrote the following aphorism, unrhymed:

> Children do not profit from their parents'
> experiences; nations do not heed history.
> The unfortunate experiences must be repeated
> ~ Over and over again.

After his wife died, he went through a terrible period of stomach problems. My father tried to find ways to ease his discomfort and once devised a special diet that he felt would help. Einstein, usually cavalier about medical advice, was appreciative of my father's efforts, and wrote to express his thanks, saying, "I am grateful . . . and now feel sincere respect both for you and for your so pertinent art in general. If there would be any relapse whatsoever on my part, please refer back to this declaration."

Later, when the pains recurred, Einstein canceled a planned social visit. Instead, he sent a letter of apology in the form of this doggerel, in which he demonstrated that, even in pain, he could retain his sense of humor:

> Alas, I cannot come to town;
> Skepticism has got me down
> Just at the moment I began
> To think your drugs could cure a man.

145

If the pain is sometimes murder
It does not drive me any further
Round the bend than I am now—
Drugs are not guilty anyhow.

In the end, the fault's my own
If maggots eat me up so soon.
You will surely understand, and give
Me your blessing when I leave.

With hearty greetings, Your Old Sinner, a.e.

So, you see, while the world admired Einstein the scientist, or chuckled at Einstein the violinist, or perhaps worried at the thought of Einstein the sailor, unprotected at sea—I, while remembering all of these aspects of the man, retain a little part of me that remembers Einstein the poet, for it was in that guise that much of Einstein's good nature came out.

CHAPTER NINE

Einstein the Musician

1. Evenings with the Violin

Despite being renowned as the greatest scientist of the twentieth century and perhaps of the past several centuries, Albert Einstein was universally recognized perhaps as much for what covered his brain as for what was in it. I am speaking, of course, of his shock of white hair that even today brings instant recognition and snickers in countless advertisements and cartoons, even among people who were not born until long after his death.

Yet, Einstein also had another defining symbol. That was the violin that he carried with him wherever he went. One of my own most endearing memories of his visits to our Manhattan home was of hearing him improvising on the violin in our kitchen—his "music studio" of choice, thanks to the ample resonance provided by the kitchen tiles. There he would play either early in the morning or late at night, often while cogitating over a particularly elusive scientific problem.

The average person, for whom even one talent in one's lifetime might seem to be more than one's share, might be in awe of a person like Einstein, who, while solving the mysteries of the universe, still found time to partake so fully of another gift such as music. But anyone who has spent time with members of the scientific community will recognize that music and science—particularly science that is steeped in mathematics, as was Einstein's—are often strongly compatible. Go to any major pharmaceutical company, for example, and the odds are that you will find among the various researchers and chemical engineers a percentage of violinists, violists, and violincellists far in excess of their normal distribution in the population. Viewed in this light, it is really only normal that Einstein, the consummate scientist, should have found such gratification in his trusty fiddle.

He often spoke to members of our family gratefully of his mother, Pauline, whose influence was paramount in directing the young Einstein toward music. At the age of six, it was arranged that Einstein should have violin lessons. His mother, a pianist herself, insisted on this. But it took Albert about seven years to become inspired by the music of Mozart, which only then instilled a new-found passion in him for the violin.

Einstein himself has told the story this way: "I took violin lessons from age six to fourteen, but had no luck with my teachers, for whom music did not transcend mechanical practicing. I really began to learn only when I was about thirteen years old, mainly after I had fallen in love with Mozart's sonatas. The attempt to reproduce, to some extent, their artistic content and their singular grace compelled me to improve my technique, which improvement I obtained from these sonatas without practicing systematically. I believe, on the whole, that love is a better teacher than sense of duty—with me, at least, it certainly was."

And so the twin interests of Einstein marched along through his formative years, the violin providing a safety valve, as it were, for the pressures of his scientific work. In later years, Hans Albert, his son, said, "Whenever he felt that he had come to the end of the road or into a difficult situation in his work, he would take refuge in music, and that would usually resolve all of his difficulties."

Einstein's love for the violin went beyond that of an avocation, almost into the realm of a vocation. Indeed, Einstein said that he had once flirted with the idea of becoming a professional violinist, and he said several times that he would have become a musician had he not succeeded in science. In an interview in the *New York Times* in 1934, he was quoted as saying that he found in music "the highest possible degree of happiness." And in *The Human Side of Albert Einstein,* he wrote: "Music does not influence research work, but both are nourished by the same source of longing, and they complement one another in the release they offer."

This complementary aspect of music and research often informed his playing. Even in his middle years in Berlin, he would often play the violin in his kitchen late at night, improvising melodies while he pondered complicated physics problems. Often when at loggerheads over a particular problem he would turn to his violin or sit at the piano (which he also played relatively well). Then, suddenly, in the middle of playing, he would announce excitedly, "I've got it!" As if by inspiration, the answer to his problem would have come to him in the midst of music.

Einstein loved to play music, both alone and with friends, but he also loved to go to concerts even more than he enjoyed going to the theater. After he married a second time and until his stepdaughter Margot got married, he would often go to concerts with her. His wife, Elsa seldom went to concerts, and that perhaps contributed to Einstein's reasons for escorting his lady friend Toni Mendel to the musical outings.

Einstein reserved most of his violin-playing for intimate evenings with friends, but he also loved to perform publicly for charity events, both in Berlin and in Princeton. After one such performance in the early 1920's in Berlin, a music critic—who, strangely enough, was not aware of his renown in physics—wrote of his playing: "Einstein's playing is excellent, but he does not deserve his world fame; there are many other violinists just as good."

Once, in Princeton, in January 1941, Einstein gave a violin recital at the Present Day Club to benefit the American Friends Service Committee, for the purpose of making clothes for refugee children in England during the war. What made this such a special event was that Einstein was accompanied on this occasion by the great French pianist Gaby Casadesus. The audience for this concert was expected to consist of many young people, since a local school was also participating in the program. But to Einstein's dismay, the audience turned out to be almost universally adult, with a heavy smattering of news reporters hungry for a glimpse of the great scientist and, of course, for a good story.

Mme Casadesus later recalled that their first offering, Mozart's Sonata #4 in E Minor, was almost scuttled. "We had so many people taking shots that at first I thought he would stop playing," she said. "But fortunately he did not. He went through playing very well and he was not disturbed."

What made this performance particularly memorable for my

family was that Einstein chose to perform also two numbers that were composed by my mother, Frieda Bucky: "Old Indian Song" and "Russian Dance."

Mme Casadesus also later commented that Einstein had played quite well on this occasion. "Don't forget to say he was a true musician," she once said. "Naturally he did not have the time to practice, so maybe he would not be able to do things that were different in technique, but, anyway, he played very well."

Those who heard Einstein play the violin generally agreed that his sense of musicality compensated for any technical deficiencies. Just as Gaby Casadesus said that he played with "marvelous phrasing and feeling," there were others who gave similar praises.

In Belgium, he had played with a Mr. Barjansky, who later wrote in a letter to Margot, "Einstein's playing of Mozart was unique. Without being a virtuoso and perhaps because of that, he reproduced the depth and the tragedy of Mozart's genius so naturally with his violin."

Einstein loved nothing better than to arrange for musical evenings with friends, who might be either amateur or professional musicians. Both in Berlin and in Princeton, he indulged this passion for chamber music evenings. On many occasions, at the Einstein home in Princeton or at one of our summer vacation spots during one of these musical get-togethers, I was privileged to attend.

At one such soiree, I witnessed one of the most famous of Einstein anecdotes and can confirm its veracity. Einstein was playing second violin in a quartet that included the great and expressive violin virtuoso Fritz Kreisler. Things were going well until, at one point, something went rhythmically awry. Suddenly Kreisler put his violin down, looked over at a perplexed Einstein, and said, "What is the matter, Professor, can't you count?" The irony of Kreisler's question, posed to the preeminent physicist of the century, brought a great round of laughter.

Not that Einstein minded being the butt of his friends' jokes. He could as easily poke fun at himself in the same situation. One of his regular quartet partners, Barbara L. Rahm (who was first violinist in an informal string quartet, with Einstein as second violinist, Alfred Hopkins as violist, and rotating guest cellists) has written, "Facetious jokes were made about Einstein's counting abilities. They were not true. He had a good sense of rhythm. However, I remember one evening when we had difficulty with a Beethoven adagio movement marked in 12/8 rhythm and usually counted in 4. I said that we should take it very slowly and count 12. Professor Einstein looked abashed and said, quite innocently, 'Oh, I don't think I can count 12.' There were guests that night and I think it afforded them some quiet amusement."

A sidelight of this quartet, as recounted by the author Jamie Sayen in his *Einstein In America,* was that Einstein, Hopkins, and Rahm all had March 14 as their birthdays, and for the three years prior to the outbreak of World War II, the group celebrated the day with dinner and chamber music.

Einstein had many musical partners, including his mother, who accompanied him in his early years on the piano; the physicist Paul Ehrenfest; Belgium's Queen Elizabeth, who was one of his closest friends; Prof. Adolf Hurwitz and his daughter; Mme Casadesus; Carola Hauschka-Spath, who was one of his Princeton neighbors, and Valentine Bargmann, one of his assistants at the Institute.

One of Einstein's closest musical attachments happened quite by accident. In Berlin, the concert pianist Joseph Schwartz was giving a recital along with his son, Boris, who was a youthful prodigy on the violin. A politician who heard them and knew of Einstein's love of the violin sent them to Einstein believing that the scientist would be very interested in hearing the young violinist.

Dutifully, Boris and his father went to Einstein's Haberland-strasse apartment. When Boris brought out his violin, he tore into Bruch's Concerto in G Minor, a virtuosic standby. When Boris reached a particularly lyrical and expressive passage in the First Movement, Einstein suddenly burst out, "Ah! One can see that he loves the violin!"

At the end of the concerto, Einstein took out his own violin and the three of them played Bach and Vivaldi trio sonatas. Einstein and the Schwartzs thus began a lasting friendship, nourished by many more such musical evenings.

Boris Schwartz himself offered another piece of the puzzle as to Einstein's violin skills. He described Einstein's tone as very pure with little vibrato. He said also that Einstein did not like the sensuous, vibrant tone that was the mainstay of nineteenth-century violinists. Schwartz added that Einstein was a good sight-reader who "played well in time," playing with tremendous concentration, leaning forward with his face practically in the music.

In his Berlin days, Einstein was a tireless violinist, ready to continue playing for hours. Often, Boris Schwartz would tire long before Einstein, and Elsa, sensing the situation, would come to the rescue, serving tea to bring an end to the music.

Even in later years in America, Einstein was ready to pick up his violin at the slightest invitation. Jamie Sayen recounts the following story in his *Einstein In America:*

Late in December 1934, when Einstein was nearly fifty-six years old, Elsa suffered an attack of sciatica. A group from the First Presbyterian Church of Princeton had a tradition of singing Christmas carols outside of the windows of local residents who were ill. So, one evening before Christmas about a dozen carolers accompanied by a violinist, Jane Lewis, assembled in front of 2 Library Place, where the Einsteins then lived. One of them described the scene this way, as Sayen reported in his book: "With snow coming down all over the place, just like an old Christmas card scene, we went over and started singing unannounced, when the front door opened and Dr. Einstein came out. He was obviously touched; he thanked us and asked if he could accompany us on our violin. We thought that was great and Jane Lewis presented him with her violin and we sang Christmas carols for quite a few minutes. He played with the snow coming down and very graciously thanked us."

By the way, thus began a tradition of serenading the Einstein home at Christmastime that continued for over fifty years, until the death of his step-daughter Margot in 1986.

Boris Schwartz's comments about Einstein's sparing use of vibrato was thoroughly in keeping with Einstein's own stated musical preferences. He was enamored of the eighteenth-century music of Bach, Vivaldi, Corelli, and Mozart, but especially of Mozart, who was his ideal. Of Mozart he liked to say that his music was so pure that it seemed to be ever-present in the universe, waiting to be discovered by Mozart. (Once, Einstein even went so far as to suggest that one of the worst consequences of atomic warfare would be that people would no longer be able to hear Mozart's music.)

In contrast, Einstein often denigrated the music of Beethoven, saying that it was obviously a personal expression of his creativity rather than a universal expression of nature as with Mozart. Particularly, he was disenchanted with Beethoven's passionate C-minor mode, which he saw as too emotionally overcharged.

In a letter to his friend the Queen Mother of Belgium in 1936, Einstein wrote, "As always, the springtime sun bursts forth new life, and we may rejoice because of this new life and contribute to its unfolding; and Mozart remains as beautiful and tender as he always was and always will be. There is, after all, something eternal that lies beyond the reach of the hand of fate and of all human delusions."

Even with Mozart, though, Einstein maintained his independence of thought. His step-daughter Margot once told of a time when he was playing a piece by Mozart on his piano. After making a mistake, he suddenly stopped and exclaimed: "Mozart wrote such nonsense here!"

In general, Einstein was not too taken with nineteenth-century composers, perhaps with the exception of Franz Schubert, who retained many of the classical structures that he cherished. In deriding nineteenth (and, certainly, twentieth) century music, Einstein was critical of its lack of formal structure. That was one of the failings for which he detested Richard Wagner, of whom he once said, "I admire Wagner's inventiveness, but I see his lack of architectural structure as decadence. Moreover, to me his musical personality is indescribably offensive so that for the most part I can listen to him only with disgust."

This was also in keeping with something that Einstein wrote in 1939 in response to a musical questionnaire. "In music, I do not look for logic," he wrote. "I am quite intuitive on the whole and know no theories. I never like a work if I cannot intuitively grasp its inner unity (architecture)."

Einstein was fortunate that he had learned to play the piano early, for as much as he loved to play the violin, he found that advancing age began to take its toll on his technique. Smooth bowing soon gave way to disturbing scratchiness, and finally, nearing the age of 70, he gave up playing the violin altogether, satisfying his musical inclinations instead on the piano.

As on the violin, Einstein would also improvise on the piano, once again demonstrating the very personal nature of his playing. Once, at my mother's home in Manhattan, Eva Kayser, Rudolf's second wife, heard Einstein improvising on the piano and tiptoed to the back of the room, hoping to listen. But, as she told it later, "Somehow he became conscious of another person being present. He looked up, saw me, and stopped immediately. I said, 'I'm very sorry, please continue.' But he wouldn't; he wasn't angry, just embarrassed. Playing was something personal."

Of his improvisations, though, Einstein in 1954 wrote to the coordinator of a group of amateur musicians at Harvard Observatory, "It is true that I have improvised much on the piano with delight, but I discovered without much astonishment that it was not worth the paper and ink to be written down."

Of course, when Einstein couldn't play music he was fortunate to benefit from the vastly improved technology of recorded music in his later years. In 1949, for his seventieth birthday, Einstein's colleagues at the Institute for Advanced Studies, led by Irwin Panofsky, decided to surprise Einstein with an FM tuner and a high-fidelity record-player. Herman Goldstine, another colleague, was chosen to secretly build the apparatus in the computer-project machine shop. All faculty members shared in the cost. On the morning of his birthday, Helen Dukas telephoned Goldstine the moment Einstein left home for his office, and he rushed over to Mercer Street to install the hi-fi system and radio antenna (as Jamie Sayen describes it, Goldstine was rewarded for his efforts with a speeding ticket on Mercer Street). Einstein was delighted by the gift, which enabled him to listen to his beloved classical music from the comfort of his home, and also helped to fill the gap created by his abandonment of the violin.

Perhaps the world owes homage as much to Einstein's love of music as to his innate scientific brilliance. For it was music, as much as anything else, that created and nourished Einstein's mental landscape, enabling it to blossom full flower into his many theories. But, perhaps even more importantly, his own performing nourished a sensitivity in Einstein's personality that shone through in all of his personal dealings. Certainly it did with my family and me.

2. Conversation: On Music

BUCKY: Many people feel as though you have the outer appearance more of a musician than of a scientist. Did you ever wish that you had taken up the violin a bit more seriously in your earlier days?

EINSTEIN: Ah, my friend, music is in my blood for sure. Unfortunately, when I was younger I did not find it too pleasurable to practice the long hours necessary to make a career of the violin. However, I was lucky to have grown up in a musical household when I lived with the Winteler family in Aarau. There, many evenings the family got together for chamber music. I got more benefit in those evenings of playing than in all of the lessons that I had to withstand as a youngster. In fact, my two major enjoyments at that time were going for long walks by myself and playing the violin.

BUCKY: Did you have a large circle of musical friends in those days?

EINSTEIN: There were quite a few of us who got together for chamber music—either as quartets, quintets, or similar groupings for sonatas. It was a circle that was ever-widening as we were always looking for more talent. This led to some interesting little situations. Once, for example, I was playing my violin when suddenly I heard someone in another apartment playing the piano. I immediately stopped playing and, taking my instrument, followed the sounds. The pianist turned out to be an elderly lady whom I had never before met and she must have been astonished because I walked right into her room and began accompanying her with my violin, saying, "Please continue to play. Don't let me disturb you." Later, my landlady told me that the old woman had gone to her and inquired, "Who is this peculiar young man?"

The landlady reassured her, telling her, "Please, don't be alarmed. He is just a harmless student that lives with me."

Another time, during one of our evenings of music, some ladies had asked to be invited to listen. They were a mother and her two daughters, I believe. These two daughters were knitting some garment all evening while we played. Well, these girls kept dropping their needles or the wool, and they would irritatingly use this excuse to whisper to each other. Finally, the distraction was too much for me and I stopped playing and put my violin back in its case. The two girls seemed surprised and asked, "Are you finished playing already?" To which I replied, "Yes, ladies, I do not think that it is right that I disturb you during your knitting."

BUCKY: Who were your favorite composers?

EINSTEIN: Mostly, I like the music of the seventeenth and eighteenth centuries. My favorites, I would say, are Vivaldi, Bach, and Mozart. But, most of all, Mozart. I think that Mozart's music is so pure and beautiful that I see it as the inner beauty of the universe, itself. And, of course, like all great beauty, his music was pure simplicity.

BUCKY: You do not include Beethoven among your favorites?

EINSTEIN: No, no. Beethoven I find much too abrupt for my tastes. And the Romantic composers are like sugar to me, much too sweet. And since the Romantics, there has been a considerable decrease in outstanding artists as far as music composers and painters are concerned.

Epilogue

People who knew Einstein as intimately as did our family were always reminded by the professor's flippant comments that to him death was just another natural phenomenon, to be awaited, expected, and observed, if such a thing were possible.

Indeed, Albert Einstein's approaching end became a kind of family drama, especially since my father was one of the three consulting physicians at his final illness. Many times, I recall my father and Einstein having deeply philosophical discussions about the nature of medicine and surgery. I will never forget when one day, after one of these conversations, Einstein laughingly rebuked my father, saying, "One can also die without the aid of a physician."

But as impending age rendered death more of a reality than a debating point, I noticed a change in Einstein's attitude. In earlier days, he feigned a total disregard of death. This blended in well with his strong belief that the problems of one person are like little fish in a big sea.

But as the end drew near, indications were that death lay heavy on his mind. At the final illness, Einstein asked his doctor whether death itself was a painful matter. What he feared most was a long, stretched-out affair.

But he still retained his charming humor about this most serious of matters. Several weeks before his death, for example, his doctor-friend Janos Plesch, visiting from Berlin, brought him a box of fine cigars, one of Einstein's weaknesses. When Einstein saw them, he smiled and said, "My God, I'll have to smoke these fast in order to enjoy them all!"

Einstein's final week was a busy one. Since Israel was celebrating its Independence Day, the Israeli Ambassador, Abba Eban, had requested that Professor Einstein participate in a special broadcast to celebrate the day. Einstein, feeling that the occasion was a momentous one, asked that the Israeli government officials assist him in drafting a statement.

Consequently, the house on Mercer Street in Princeton saw a flurry of prestigious visitors, including Abba Eban himself and the Israeli consul, Reuven Dafni. (During their visit, exactly one week before Einstein's death, Mr. Eban told the professor that, through the new technology of television, he would be seen and heard by some sixty million people. Einstein characteristically remarked, laughing, "You see, I still might become world famous, after all!")

But underneath the surface of all the activity, the scientist's body was suffering. The heart that had supported the brilliance of the great physicist was giving out. Specifically, Einstein's aorta was bursting, the resultant internal bleeding sapping him of energy, and, ultimately, of life.

On the thirteenth of April, 1955, Einstein's tiredness led to his collapsing. His secretary had to handle the situation on her own since Einstein's step-daughter Margot was herself in the hospital in Princeton for convalescence.

It was on the next day that my father was called in, along with a cardiac surgeon, Dr. Frank Glenn, and a Dr. Ehrmann. A decision had to be reached quickly as to whether or not to operate on Einstein, who was now in his seventy-seventh year. But Einstein was violently opposed to surgery. (He had indicated to me in private conversation that one reason he didn't totally trust medical tinkering with the body was that, unlike his own science, there could be no stock mathematical equations or formulas to govern success.) And the surgeons themselves could only guarantee a fifty-fifty chance of success based upon Einstein's advanced age and the fledgling state of this kind of surgery.

After teetering between worsening and improving, Einstein was finally moved to the Princeton Hospital. These last couple of days, it was evident that Einstein was dying. My family visited the hospital each day. As usual, Einstein was patient, accepting his impending death with equanimity.

On the night he died, we were all visiting at his bedside. I still remember his humor, even at that late hour. As my father was saying goodbye, Einstein asked him, "Why are you going so soon?" My father answered him, saying, "Because you should go to sleep." Smiling, Einstein said, "Gustav, you don't have to leave. Your presence does not stop me from falling asleep."

They were, fatefully, the last words that Einstein was ever to speak to any of our family. We all left the hospital and returned to our apartment in the Hotel Carlyle in Manhattan, where we were living at the time. At approximately 1:15 A.M. the next morning, 18 April 1955, the telephone jarred us out of a gentle sleep. It was Hans Albert Einstein, calling to inform us that his father had died only minutes before.

That morning, I telephoned Daniel Brigham, a reporter for the *New York Journal-American,* with the news of Einstein's death, thus becoming the conduit for this information of international import to be made public.

It is one of history's little misfortunes that, at the moment of his death, Einstein was mumbling something in his native tongue. His attending nurse, Alberta Roszel, unfortunately didn't understand German, so Einstein's final words were forever lost.

Years before, my father had said that "hurry and tension and anything infringing on concentration was like a bodily pain to him." But now there would be no more hurrying and no more tension. For Einstein was at last at peace.

He had set certain ground rules for his funeral. There was to be a lapse of several hours before the press was informed so that few people would have time to travel to his funeral, which was to be held the same day. Consequently, the world did not learn of the great scientist's passing until approximately 9:30 the following morning. He was to be cremated and his ashes distributed to the wind, so that no one would have an opportunity to idolize his grave.

So it was that at 4:00 P.M. on the eighteenth of April, eleven people gathered in Ewing, New Jersey, near Princeton for the cremation ceremonies. A mark of the closeness of our family to this remarkable man was that almost one-half of the attendees— four of the ten—were Buckys, including myself. It was one of the simplest and most touching funerals that I have ever witnessed.

I still could not fathom the fact that this man, with whom I had spent so many stimulating and wonderful years, was gone. To me, he had almost seemed like a supernatural being who could never die.

Was, indeed, Einstein's intellect supernatural? Or was it just good fortune or a phenomenon explainable by natural causes? There have been opportunities for study, beginning with Einstein's autopsy, when his brain was given over to Tom Harvey, a pathologist now living in Weston, Missouri.

Studies have been as crude as measuring the size of the brain (which revealed it to be, indeed, larger than average). And they have been as sophisticated as a study undertaken by Marian Diamond, a neuroanatomist, some years ago in Berkeley, California, who got samples of Einstein's brain from Dr. Harvey. Diamond and his co-workers decided to study sections of the upper front and lower rear of both hemispheres (areas that are involved in "higher" thinking, i.e., associating and analyzing information received from the sensory parts of the brain).

The scientists looked at the ratio of two kinds of brain cells—neurons and glial cells. (Neurons, which cannot divide, are the basic cells of the brain; glial cells, which *can* increase in number, provide support and nourishment to the neurons.) Diamond's previous work had shown that animals placed in environments that stimulate mental activity develop more glial cells per neuron. Therefore, the scientists hypothesized that Einstein's brain might contain more than the normal number of glial cells. Indeed, tests proved them to be correct—Einstein's brain contained more glial cells per neuron in all four areas, compared with the brains of eleven normal males, aged 47 to 80. But the differences were statistically significant only in the samples from the left rear portion.

Commenting on the research, Diamond said, "We do not know if Einstein was born with this or developed it in later years. But it tells us that in one of the highest evolved areas of the brain, there is evidence that he had greater intellectual processing."

It is satisfying to reflect upon the fact that all of Einstein's wishes were adhered to after his death. His cremation left no touristy gravesite for adoring throngs. And even to this day Einstein's home at 112 Mercer Street in Princeton has not been turned into a museum or a flocking place for the masses. Einstein would, indeed, be pleased.

Einstein's Legacy

Albert Einstein was one of the two or three greatest physicists the world has ever known. In his honor, an element (einsteinium) and a unit of measurement (the einstein) have been named. He was, of course, primarily a theoretician, and that in extremely difficult subjects. When I was a young man it was a commonplace (although inaccurate) saying that only twelve people in the world could understand his theory of relativity.

What is not so well known is that he had a great appreciation of the real world in which we all live, and had the extraordinary ability of creating theories which gave us new ways of looking at that world and understanding it better. It is true that many thousands of scientists have worked on expanding Einstein's theories; but it is also true that the practical consequences of his work have changed your world and mine in almost countless ways. Just one small example: the automated checkout devices in supermarkets would not be possible without just one of Einstein's theories.

Let us list some of Einstein's major theoretical accomplishments, and then see to what changes in our own world some of these have led.

The special theory of relativity.

The equivalence of mass and energy.

The general theory of relativity.

The photon theory of light.

The basic theories of photochemistry and photoelectricity.

The theory of Brownian motion and diffusion.

The theory of specific heats of matter.

The first known laws of quantum theory.

When Einstein completed his academic studies in 1905, he was unable to find a position in science; the best job he could get was as an examiner of patent applications. But in that same year he burst upon the world of science with four theoretical papers, each of which contained a great discovery in physics.

Einstein's later work was largely the development of these basic ideas. These were the *special theory of relativity,* with the startling idea that two people could measure the same thing at the same time with complete precision and get two different results; the *theory of Brownian motion,* through which for the first time one could observe through a microscope the impact of single molecules; the *theory of the equivalence of mass and energy,* the basis for all nuclear energy; and the foundation of the *photon theory of light,* showing that light consists of extremely tiny particles.

All of these theories seem to fly in the face of common sense, and there was no conclusive experimental evidence that any of them were true; this came later, and in the case of the equivalence of mass and energy direct evidence came much later with the demonstration of the energy released from the conversion of mass to energy through nuclear fission. But all of them have had great consequences, not only for theoretical physics but also in their practical consequences for all of us.

Let us briefly review four of Einstein's great contributions to science, with an indication only at this point as to their practical importance.

The General Theory of Relativity. Arising from the special theory of relativity, the General Theory was a whole new framework for science from the extremely small (sub-molecular level) to the extremely large (the entire universe). It included a new law of gravitation, replacing Newton's law stated in the 1600's. Conclusions reached from Einstein's relativity theories are that nothing can exceed the speed of light; that the mass of an object increases as the object moves faster; that the universe is four-dimensional rather than three-dimensional, and is curved in the presence of mass, and that gravity is actually a consequence of motion in this curved space-time continuum.

There are remarkable consequences to the theory of relativity. Consider the problem of sending a space ship to another star than our own. If nothing can exceed the speed of light, neither can a spaceship go any faster than light, stringently limiting our ability to visit even stars comparatively close to us. (This has caused science fiction writers a lot of trouble!) On the other hand, consider a machine which accelerates atomic particles to high speeds. As the particle goes faster and faster, it gets heavier and heavier, making it harder and harder to accelerate; as its velocity approaches the speed of light, a particle which is one of the lightest objects in the universe at rest gets heavy enough to have very perceptible effects if it runs into another particle at high speed, perhaps even to smash an atom into bits. This is the basis for the atom smashers found in all highly developed countries, and also for a machine called a betatron, which is used for treating cancer.

The equivalence of mass and energy. Most of us are familiar with the famous formula $E = m c$ squared. This formula states that a mass m is equivalent to an amount of energy equal to the mass times the square of the speed of light. Until the discovery of nuclear fission by Lise Meitner and Otto Hahn in the 1930's, this equivalence was largely of theoretical interest, but the discovery that when an atom was split an enormous amount of energy was released made the mass-energy equivalence of enormous, even terrifying, practical importance. Nuclear bombs depend on the conversion of mass to huge amounts of energy, but so do nuclear power plants.

The photon theory of light: photochemistry and photoelectricity. Einstein, leaning on the pioneering work of Max Planck was the first to propose that light actually consisted of extremely small particles. But Einstein went further and defined the basic principles by which light interacts with matter. He received the Nobel prize for this work, not (as many think) for his theory of relativity.

The consequences of Einstein's photoelectric theory have been so widespread as to make it difficult to list all of the science that depends on this theory. For example, although photographs had been taken before Einstein's work, they were very crude, and there was no theory that could be used in designing photographic films. Einstein's work created the theoretical basis for photochemistry (using light in chemical reactions) and photoelectricity (using light to produce electricity, or electricity to produce light directly rather than by heated wires).

163

The theory of Brownian motion and diffusion. The English botanist Robert Brown noticed in 1827 that under a microscope, small grains of pollen in water moved continually and erratically without any discernible cause. This was a curiosity for the scientific world, and a number of other scientists investigated this effect without finding out why small particles in water always showed this apparently random motion. Einstein suspected that the motion was actually caused by the random bombardment of the particles by the extremely minute molecules of water itself. This was an interesting finding, but Einstein went further in investigating the fundamental laws that underlie the effect. He derived a theoretical treatment of *diffusion,* a word that includes both the transport of material in liquids from one place to another, and the transport of heat through a heat-conducting medium.

Problems of diffusion occur in many applications of chemical engineering to chemical reactions, as well as in problems of heat transfer. Your author used this theory in a computer model of a Florida river to help determine how much fresh water could be withdrawn from a river for municipal water supply without having salt water diffuse so far upstream as to damage the environment. Heat exchangers such as car radiators all are based on the diffusion process.

We list now a number of items in ordinary use that depend on Einstein for their theoretical basis. Naturally, a number of other scientists and engineers carried these items through to their present state, but they are all based on Einstein's theories.

HOUSEHOLD:

Fluorescent lights (photoelectricity)

Night lights that go on when the house lights are turned off (photoelectricity)

Exterior lights that go on when the sun goes down (photoelectricity)

Home security systems that depend on the breaking of a light or infrared beam (photoelectricity)

Television (photoelectricity)

CD disc players (photoelectricity)

Remote controls for TV, VCR, etc. (photoelectricity)

Day-glow paints (photon theory)

Devices that use light-emitting diodes (LEDs)
(photoelectricity), including:

    Microwave Ovens
    Electric Stoves
    Radios
    TV sets
    Calculators
    Automobile dashboard indicators

Air Conditioning (diffusion)

Refrigerator (diffusion)

CAMERAS:

Automatic exposure cameras (photoelectricity, Bucky/Einstein
Patent. In his entire life, Einstein only applied for one patent.
The application was a joint one, with Dr. Gustav Bucky as co-
inventor, and was applied for in 1936. Bucky and Einstein invented the first device for automatically controlling the exposure given by a camera according to the surrounding light
level.)

Exposure meters (photoelectricity)

Photographic film (photochemistry)

Photographic print paper (photochemistry)

IN THE DOCTOR'S OFFICE:

Fluoroscopy (photoelectricity)

Image intensifiers (photoelectricity)

X-Ray intensifying screens (photoelectricity)

X-Ray film (photochemistry)

Film badges (photochemistry)

Electron beam therapy for cancer patients (Special theory of relativity)

Cobalt gamma-ray therapy for cancer patients (mass-energy equivalence, photon theory)

Radioisotope therapy for cancer patients (mass-energy equivalence)

Detection of cancer by radioisotope scans (mass-energy equivalence, photon theory)

CAT scanners for visualizing the inside of the body (photon theory)

Nuclear magnetic resonance scanners for visualizing the inside of the body (photon theory)

Echocardiogram scanners for visualizing the inside of the heart (photon theory)

Laser surgery (photon theory)

Scanners for visualizing the inside of the esophagus, stomach, bowels and abdomen (photon theory)

IN THE SUPERMARKET:

Freezers (diffusion)

Refrigerators (diffusion)

Checkout counter automatic belt stop (photoelectricity)

Checkout counter laser scanner (photoelectricity)

Fluorescent lights (photoelectricity)

NUCLEAR ENERGY:

Nuclear reactors (mass-energy equivalence)

Nuclear-powered power plants (mass-energy equivalence)

Nuclear-powered ships (mass-energy equivalence)

Nuclear-powered satellites (mass-energy equivalence)

Thermoluminescent radiation dosimeters (photoelectricity)

Film radiation badges (photochemistry)

Geiger counter (photon theory, photoelectricity)

COMPUTERS:

Monitor screens (photoelectricity)

Laser printers (photoelectricity)

LED indicator lights (photoelectricity)

MILITARY:

Atomic and hydrogen bombs (mass-energy equivalence)

Electronic display devices (photoelectricity)

Night vision scanners (photoelectricity)

Laser-guided missiles (photoelectricity)

WILLIAM M. SILER

(Dr. Siler, an expert in mathematical models of biological and hydrodynamic systems, is a senior research associate at the Mote Marine Laboratory in Sarasota, Fla.)

Index